The Second Coming

Youssef Khalim

ISBN:978-0-9787798-0-1
ISBN-13: 978-0978779801

DEDICATION

To: Lori (The real or ideal soul mate: inspiration)

Tonya Tracy Khalim and

Runako Soyini Khalim, (my most beloved daughters)

Mother and Grandmother and Great-grandmother, (my most beloved maternal biological ancestors, and spiritual antecedents)

M. A. Garvey (one of my 7 M's: my role models)

Youssef Khalim II; III (my most beloved sons)

Father and Grandfather and Great-grandfather, (my most beloved paternal biological ancestors, and spiritual antecedents).

To: The Forerunners and Reincarnation sources (beloved biological ancestors and spiritual antecedents), and

The Almighty (our Spiritual Father), from whence we come.

CONTENTS

I.   ACKNOWLEDGMENTS

To: The Forerunners and Reincarnation sources (beloved biological ancestors and spiritual antecedents), and

The Almighty (our Spiritual Father), from whence we come.

II. INTRODUCTION

The Second Coming is something momentous, something apocryphal. It is the biography of a very ordinary person- who may not be quite so ordinary after all. Imagine that *this* is you:

You are a down-to-earth, upstanding person, with integrity, and a genuine sense of justice. You believe in truth, beauty, science, order in the universe, and moral correctness. You were born into a Christian family, but at the age of 14, you begin the study all major religions, including Christianity, Judaism, Islam, Buddhism, Shinto, and Hinduism. At about the age of 20, you embrace Islam. At the age of 27, you begin the practice of Yoga and Kabala. And on July 20, 1980, you obtain Unity.

On 5/2/2000, you are writing *The Resurrection of Noah*, which is about "how life works," how the birth and death of souls works, and what the "Bibles" say about reincarnation. Based on many verses in the Qur'an and the Bible, you have a suspicion that the Prophet Muhammad may be the reincarnation of Moses. You plan a meditation session, (a "conscious," though immobile state) to research the matter. And you carefully formulate the question that you will ask. You successfully go into meditation. And you experience this:

First, there are the sights and sounds of mighty, swirling winds, and sand, in the desert. Then, the sands morph into a face!

"Is Prophet Muhammad the reincarnation of Moses?" You ask. The winds stop swirling, and the sands stand still.

"Of course," it says. And you are amazed!

Earlier, on August 4, 1999, you are in the process of writing explanations about how reincarnation works, regarding the same book (The Resurrection of Noah). At about 10:30 PM, you are lying in bed and you think: Wouldn't it be cool if I could write a story on any of my (supposed) incarnations, or others where I was "famous" – and sell it.

You have this experience: Your "consciousness" goes back to 1955, and then to Jefferson Elementary School, the first school you attended in Chicago. You wonder what this means.

You start researching Thomas Jefferson, on the Internet, and in your home Encyclopedias. Amazingly, at about 1:54 AM, you receive an email from a guy named Jefferson (Jefrsn@aol.com) *while you are researching Jefferson*. You tell Jefferson about this synchronicity. You tell him your question, and about your quest.

Finally, you write an email to Jeannette DeLangis, a "Psychic Hostess," on AOL, asking her the same question,

"Am I the Reincarnation of Thomas Jefferson?

On August 5, 1999, at about 11:46 AM, you go into meditation.

You ask, "Am I the Reincarnation of Thomas Jefferson?"

A display "window" appears. The "Yes" response (answer) is clicked.

On 2/23/2002, you discover that Thomas Jefferson is/was the reincarnation of Jacob.

Again, in meditation you ask, "Was Thomas Jefferson the reincarnation of Jacob, father of the 12 boys who became known as the Nation of Israel?" The display "window" appears. The "Yes" response (answer) is clicked.

Your Birth:

Just moments after your umbilical cord is cut: You raise your head up high and look all around the room. Side-to-side, you look - all around the room! You lower yourself back down. Then, you do it again! The people in the room are astonished!

In June, 2008, you have a dream indicating that Barack Obama is the reincarnation of President Abraham Lincoln.

Your goal is to recombine Judaism, Christianity, and Islam back into one faith. Just as Thomas Jefferson set forth the ideals, foundation, and ideology of the previous 240 years, your goal in this life cycle is to begin to set forth the ideals, foundation, ideology, and institutions for the Millennium – the Second Coming, also called the Resurrection.

You should tell your story. Write your autobiography.

The Second Coming is the autobiography of Youssef Khalim. He spent the first 11 years of his life in Mississippi. Then, he and his family moved to Chicago where he attended, first, Thomas Jefferson Elementary School, and lastly, DeVry University.

Almost immediately after practicing Yoga and Kabala, Youssef was able to "see" on the other side, in visions, dreams, and during Astral travels.

The autobiography is largely about what he saw, and what it means. But, it is also about his quest, study, research, and experiences that have produced his stark determinations and conclusions.

iii

Youssef believes *The Second Coming* started during the Clinton administration. He believes that these times complete the cycle starting with "Adam," and God begins to fully re-establish His sovereignty over the earth.

It is a time when science, technology, and innovation create the conditions for "heaven on earth," and when those conditions and individuals in opposition to truth, justice, caring, sharing, openness, and privacy will not exist on earth. *The Second Coming* has enormous implications for the political, military, economic, and social history of the USA - and for the future of the world. The book is full of useful information, hopeful ideology, and is part of an evolving blueprint for action, and the establishment of the real New World Order.

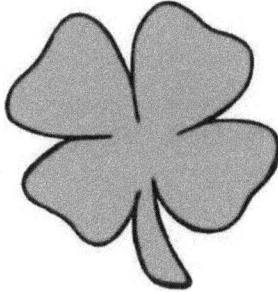

III. THE COMPLETION OF CYCLES AND SEEDS

(A Partial Biological Lineage of the Khalim's in the Present Lifecycle)

-Noah Patrick Khalim is the seed of Kathleen Mary and Youssef Khalim; born 3-17-94, in Chicago, Illinois.

-Youssef Khalim is the seed of Ruby Lee Watson and Samuel Albert Green; born 6-3-44, in Cleveland, Miss.

-Samuel Albert Green is the seed of Mary Costley and John Green; born 2-22-1909, in Cary, Miss.

-Ruby Lee Watson is the seed of Annie Shinault and Charles Watson; born 1-26-1921, in Shaw, Miss.

-John Green was born to Annie Highland and Lewis Green on 12-2-1878, in Vicksburg, Miss. Lewis Green was born in 1855, in South Carolina.

-Mary Costley is the seed of Martha Costley and Ira Costley; born 11-23-1889. The 1900 Census indicates Mary's birth year as 1886. Ira Costley was born in 1859, Martha, in 1864.

-Charles Watson is the seed of Bessie Mays Watson and Matthew Watson; born in 1893, in Duck Hill, Miss. Matthew Watson is listed in the 1840 and 1845 Mississippi Census.

-Annie Shinault is the seed of Katie Berry and James Shinault; born 4-11-1889, near Greenville, Miss.

-James Shinault was born in 1864 to Lizzie Shinault. Tradition says Lizzie was born in Virginia. The census shows 1852, in North Carolina.

-Katie Berry is the seed of Margaret Berry and Sandy Berry, born in 1862. She lived in Humphrey/Hines County, Miss. Sandy Berry was born in 1831.

-Bessie Mays Watson was born to Tina Mays.

1 THE SECOND COMING

It's so good to be alive again, forever and ever more! And since I've come back for the very last time, it is... The Second Coming!

My grandmother cut the cord. She and others cleaned me up. Then, I "raised my head up high and looked all around the room. Side-to-side, I looked-all around the room! I lowered myself back down. Then, I did it again!" My Mom, grandmother (Big Mama), Aunt Hattie, and her husband (Uncle Will) witnessed this event. And they were astonished!

So, I was born in Cleveland, Mississippi, near a farming community, on June 3, 1944, at about 9:20 PM.

Big Mama, a professional midwife, "brought" me into the world this time. Her real name is Annie Watson. I feel special, grateful, and fortunate to have had my very own grandmother cut the cord, so I could finally breathe - and live. And it's good to be alive!

My earliest remembrance is of a time when I was about four years old. My family lived in the eighth house of a row of about eight houses, in The Brickyard, an urban area, of Cleveland, Mississippi. I remember my mother, our house, and a visitor we had at that time.

The Cleveland environment was ideal in many ways. It was a mix of urban, suburban, and country lifestyles, all kind of overlapping. I also remember my great grandmother, Katie Shinault, who lived with Big Mama. And, I don't ever remember seeing Grandma Katie when she was not sitting.

In the Brickyard, we (my grandmother) had fig trees, and peach trees. Nearby, there were pecan trees, and forested areas, farmland, and a bayou. Fishing was available in the nearby bayou, on the way to downtown. The area across the road, opposite the row of houses where we lived, was an open field, and was alternately used to grow crops, or for other purposes.

My grandmother once rented a section of it, which she fenced-off, and raised and maintained a bull for slaughter, and for food.

When I got old enough to go to school, I went to the school down-town. And the way we traveled downtown to school was to walk on the railroad-track ties, and to follow the tracks, to downtown. The Brickyard was considered too close to downtown to be serviced by a school bus at that time.

I don't remember having much conversation with my great-grand-mother, Grandma Katie. But I do remember when she died, in 1952, (reputedly) at the age of 106. And, I remember many, many people coming from near and far to be at her funeral.

1

In about 1953, my family lived on the Fredrick's Plantation, near the Brickyard. And during this time, I learned to ride a bike. And it was so cool to ride on the "Blacktop" road, pumping that bike, going as fast as possible, then coasting, gliding, soaring - the wind in my face! And then, doing it all over again!

Then, there was hardly ever any automobile traffic on the Blacktop road, and I remember seeing as much farm equipment vehicle traffic on this road, as automobiles. I believe this Blacktop road is now called Chrisman Road.

I remember a girl of interest and involvement at this time. We called her Poochy. And I'm mentioning this because females have always been a central and pivotal factor in my life, as you will see later.

In Cleveland, my Uncle Will worked at the cement factory.

Other major sources of employment in the town included the ice house, the seed and grain store, the cotton gin, the furniture store, a hotel, a college, three movie theaters, the scrap and iron reclamation company, the Post Office, the lumberyard, the train, the bus company, the jail, 3 cab companies, a fire house, two 5 & Dime stores, 5 funeral homes, the RC Nehi Bottling Company, 3 doctors' offices, and the Board of Health Clinic.

There was a radio station, owned by an African American. And he also owned a cleaners, and The Booker-T Theater, one of three in Cleveland.

Downtown, we had a number of grocery stores, and I remember visiting the Italian and Chinese grocery stores, on the weekend, when our family went downtown. I remember the cool, insatiably delicious ice cream, at the Ice Cream Parlor.

Once we lived on a farm, in Merrigold. And I remember riding on somebody's bull, at least several times. I remember a boy, (Sam) drowning in a nearby pond. And I remember shooting marbles, and playing with the toy hauling and lifting trucks that Fred, my older brother and I had gotten for Christmas. I remember how cold our house would be, in the morning, before one of us got up, and started a fire in our heating stove.

In Cleveland, one Christmas, in about 1949, I stayed up late, and helped my Mom with the cooking. And I got to lick the cake batter from the stirring spoons. I helped prepare the "stockings" for the other children, consisting of huge brown paper bags, filled with apples, oranges, nuts, and candy. All of these goodies, candies, fruits, and cooked foods made the most delicious, wonderful, and pleasant smells you could ever imagine!

As usual, we put the Christmas presents by the Christmas tree. And I think I remember someone getting a bike for Christmas.

I remember Uncle Will letting me drive his automobile, for a short distance, in Cleveland. We were so lucky! Uncle Will and Aunt Hattie too, always treated me, and my Mom's children, like Little Princes and Princesses. Aunt Hattie, just like Aunt Bessie, never had her own children. Each occasionally asked my Mom to give them one or more of us.

Here, I want to tell you something: I remember cranking cars, by hand. Yes, we would take out the crank, go in front, by the radiator, and crank the car, to start it, in about 1953!

I remember driving someone's automobile for a short distance, in 1953, when we lived in Shaw, Mississippi.

1.1 Summary of Events From Age 7-10:

At the age of seven, I used to clean and maintain the house, and do some cooking while the adults, or older people tilled or harvested the crops. I collected eggs from our own and other peoples' chickens. I also gathered foods such as berries, okra, pecans, pears, peaches, plums, melons, tomatoes, and persimmons for the family. I fished, and helped take care of the family pets. I also fed the family animals that were maintained for food.

At about the age of nine and ten, I used to hire-out to till or harvest crops for other farmers. I would also gather firewood, chop down trees, plow the fields, run errands, operate a "trout-line" in the bayou, catch fish, edible turtles and frogs, and gather water from outdoor pumps.

At about the age of 10, I could carry a sack of cotton weighing well over 100 pounds. And I harvested corn, cotton, and other products.

1953:

In about 1953-54, the older children: Dorothy, Fred, and I used to get hired out to plantation owners, to make some extra cash. We would get up very, very early, way before daylight. We called this "Day Labor Work," and we used to chop (and weed) cotton, or pick cotton, or corn, and till, or harvest other crops. We would use money made from this work to buy clothes, food, or for other needs.

In Drew, Mississippi, when we lived on the Bud Bishop Plantation, my experiences were very sweet and dear, reminding me of the fables about Tom Sawyer, and Huckleberry Finn. Bud Bishop had a daughter, Catherine, who had polio. Fred and I used to go up to the Bishop house and get eggs, handed to us by Catherine. [Note: Please remember the

3

names Bishop and Catherine. And think about how patterns are repeated, over and over in life. I will show you how those *names* relate to my life, and my story, later.]

Ours was a farmhouse, adjacent to a deep and narrow stream, which emptied down into the bayou. We walked on a wooden, semi-flexible walkway-bridge (of planks) from one side to the other.

We had several pear trees adjacent to the storage barn. And we had several pecan trees, down, away from the house, and on either side of the stream. We boys had numerous trees available for climbing! But we usually climbed them to gather pecans, peaches, or pears. We would climb the tree and shake the limbs and branches to make the pecans, pears, or peaches fall to the ground. In the case of the pears, we'd make them fall to the ground or onto the roof of the adjacent barn. A pasture separated our house from the bayou. In the spring and summer, the bayou would often fill to the brim with sparkling waters, and fish, and turtles, and frogs.

Uncle Son, and Aunt Bessie lived about two blocks away. Uncle Son was an avid hunter, fisherman, and a good storyteller. He used to get a kick out of telling us what some of his other nephews or nieces had done, or about his fishing, farming, and hunting adventures! He had many nieces and nephews, besides my Mom's children.

Uncle Son used to maintain a "Trout Line" in the bayou. And it was a great treat to go out with him to his line, in his boat, and see the catfish or perch he had caught overnight. Riding in the boat was a very exciting, and cool experience. We would ride down narrow passageways, often numerous tree limbs and branches at arm's length, making turns, and navigating cautiously through these passageways. Sometimes, we would see frogs, or maybe snakes scurrying back into the water. And we could hear the various birds, singing: Robins, Woodpeckers, Blue Jays, Owls, and Black Birds.

As I said, Aunt Bessie never had her own children, and she used to spoil us, and treat me, and my Mom's children like Princes and Princesses. We were altogether catered to, and pampered. She would serve us her finest foods and drinks, sometimes taking out delicacies that had been stored away. She would give us gifts, like clothes, toys, or food. And when we stayed over, she would tell us interesting stories, and later, she would tuck us into her warm, clean, soft, and luxurious guest bed.

Uncle Son and Aunt Bessie would share canned foods, game animals, (got through Uncle Son's hunting or fishing) and store bought products. Across the Walkway Bridge, the Bud Bishop plantation maintained a pasture of numerous goats, pigs, and cattle. And he sold milk, eggs, and butter. He also had a grocery store.

4

In Drew, we went to school in the building which also served as the home for New Hope Baptist Church. And this is when I began to learn how to read, through The Dick and Jane Reader. I also learned to read through studying and preparing for Sunday School Lessons.

I was seven years old when I got baptized. I remember the light blue suit of the Minister, and the amazing light blue water!

At church, I had my first crush on a girl, Evon Staples.

In Drew, children and adults used to gather black berries, persimmons, plums, apples, okra, watermelons, and cantaloupes, much of which just grew "wild:" Apple trees were on the "Ella Zima" plantation. The plum trees were on the Bishop plantation. The other foods would just be scattered about, in patches, or randomly, in the fields, or along the roads.

What did we play with? We often made our own toys. We made balls, out of cloth and rubber bands. For a bat, a suitable tree limb, cut and pruned, fit the bill! We sometimes just rolled tires, pushing them ahead, very fast, or slowly, rounding corners, controlling the movement. We also played marbles. We played with store bought toys: trucks and hauling and construction equipment. We sometimes rode bulls, mules, or horses for fun, or we used them to make trips, or run errands.

I was good with my fists, and my cousin, Chuck, and his friends, Bernard and Willie Williams, and maybe "Ball," who were several years older than me, used to put me up to fight boys about my age. And I could beat everyone they put me up against! Now this wasn't as barbaric as it might seem. The "warriors" would aim body-shots at each other, and it was only when, or if a "warrior" got really upset, that he might go all out, and try to really hurt the other guy.

Also, I could always out-box my brother, Fred, even though he was much bigger than me, and exactly 1.5 years older than me. As long as I stayed on the outside, within arm's length, fists flying, I could win! But, Fred used to win by getting on the inside, grabbing me, and giving me a bear hug, and I couldn't move! This would make me so angry! And I would scream, cry, and fight like the dickens, to get free from him!

In 1955, my family lived on the Hitch's Plantation. And Fred and I were visiting a creek to gather oysters, and the creek was adjacent to the house of two boys that we sometimes played with: William, and I don't remember the other boy's name.

William and I were doing more wrestling than gathering oysters. He was sweaty, bothersome, and persistent. It was hot! I would beat him, subdue him, but he kept coming back for more! And he was very annoying and aggravating to me. Somehow, and somewhere, in his house, I got a dull, but dangerous knife. And I cut him, somewhere about his forehead. I would

5

teach him a lesson! He bled like crazy! I was scared. We children tried to bandage his head up!

But, the bandage became bloody, the blood soaked through, very red, and threatening! And the adults, and finally, the plantation owner got involved in this affair. There was a suggestion, or threat of getting the Sheriff involved, and or disciplining me in some way.

Then, on August 24, 1955, Emmet Till, from Chicago, age 14, and another teenage boy, were visiting a grocery store in the small nearby town of Money, Mississippi. Emmet was brutalized and murdered by the anti-African American terrorists, J. W. Milam and Roy Bryant, his half-brother. They accused Emmet of making a pass (whistling) at Roy's wife, Carolyn, while in the store. The incident with William, the hope of better financial prospects, and the Emmet Till murder convinced my Mom and Step-dad, Jimmy Anderson, to leave the south for good, and to come to Chicago.

We already had some relatives in Chicago: Aunts, Uncles, and cousins. Actually, my step-dad, Jimmy Anderson, arrived in Chicago prior to the Emmet Till murder, which was not discovered until August 31, 1955.

1.2 I Arrived in Chicago

I arrived in Chicago on the Greyhound Bus, just after Thanksgiving Day, in 1955. It was great looking out the window on the way here, and watching the countryside: forests, farms, animals, houses, long stretches of flat lands, and open lands. At the rest stations, I saw greeting cards, gifts, maps, and memorabilia. I watched the people, getting on and off the bus.

I came to Chicago with my Mom, and Fred. The rest of our family was already here: Jimmy Anderson, and his son, Ivory, had arrived in August. Dorothy had brought with her, James and Bobbie, two younger siblings.

I was impressed with the escalators at the Greyhound Bus Depot, seen for the very first time. I played on them, going up-and-down them some. The Greyhound Bus Station was then located on Randolph Street, between Dearborn, and Clark St.

We left the bus station in a relative's automobile. Subsequently, we lived with my Aunt Annie Mae (and Big Mama), at the Terminal Hotel, 1722 W. Roosevelt Road, Chicago.

Across the street, there were two movie theaters. The Central Park was directly across from the hotel, and there was another one, The Broadway Strand, in the next block, east.

Soon, some boys were picking on my brother, Fred. And Fred and I met them, across the street, in front of the Central Park Theater. I took the bigger one. I out-boxed him! I kicked his butt! And he later became friends with my brother and me.

At the age of 11, (in Chicago) I changed my name from "Jimmie" to James, on my own, and without any consultation with anyone. Also, I operated a snowball wagon, and sold snowball cones. And I earned money by doing odd jobs for relatives, especially Aunt Hattie.

In 1955, Fred was 12 years old, and he got a job, and he always kept a job – until he became disabled, in about 1990. First, Fred worked in a Drug Store. Then, he shined shoes. In his teen years, he worked at Kopper Kettle, downtown. When he was about 17, he went into the Army. When he came out, in about 1962, he worked for CTA, then Shell.

Fred died in 1999, a victim of our social, political, educational, and economic system; he became an adversary to himself. Earlier, he always worked too much. And he did not get the education and training, and a reflective, healthy lifestyle that could have prolonged his life, or change the quality of his life for the better. But, while he was with us, he tried to always convene us. He always thought of us as a family, and extended family, and as Americans, sharing and caring for each other.

Ok. Back to my story: Going east from the Terminal Hotel, there were many stores on our side (north side) of the street, a 5 & Dime Woolworth Store, shops, meat markets, and clothing stores.

I first attended Thomas Jefferson Elementary School, located at 1522 W. Fillmore Ave. It was exactly two blocks east, and one block north of our hotel! (Are we beginning to see symbolic *synchronicities* here?) Much more, later!

I remember excelling in doing my Time Tables. I remember demonstrating my ability at the blackboard, showing off, doing Time Tables through 13 and 14. And I remember my teacher, a beautiful, slim, and shapely African American woman, with grey eyes. Do all (country) boys, age 11, remember their first lovely and attractive teacher with love, affection, and adoration?

I remember doing homework assignments. Some really stick out. I used to have to get stories, with a newspaper graphic (photo) out of the Chicago American Newspaper. I would tape the photo to writing paper, and summarize the contents in my own words, below, or to one side. I (we) used to get a School Newsletter, or Weekly Reader, which was about events from all over the world.

And I remember doing a graphic, based on the National Anthem, and drawing rockets, red flares, cannon, flags, and the battle scenes, and troops fighting! And this memory still makes a very great impression on me, and it grabs me profoundly, throughout my mind, heart, and soul.

7

Anyway, back to Jefferson Elementary School. Well, (What else?) we used to box and fight, during recess, going from end to end (east to west) in the schoolyard. Some of what we did almost seems like forming a line, like football players, and fighting our way to the end zone. But, we would just be fighting (boxing) with each other.

I remember a boyhood friend from the time, Raymond. He lived in the then, nice Projects, near Ashland and Roosevelt Road.

I attended Grant School for a short time. Then, I attended Gladstone Elementary School, at Washburn and Damen Ave.

At Gladstone, some of my friends included Milton (and Eddie) Williams, Thomas Blackman, Larry (Lawrence and his brother, Errol) Griffin, Judy, Gladys, and Gee Wilson. Sorry, I don't remember some of your last names, guys.

Gladstone was where I really got into reading. One teacher, Mr. Cutt, had lists and lists of books that were suggested or assigned to us. And I read just about all the Classics, including Tom Sawyer, Huckleberry Finn, Black Beauty, First and Ten, etc., etc. Mr. Cutt used to stand at the top of the stairs, looking like he was in control of the whole world, sort of wiggling a leg, like Elvis Presley used to do, (as children came into school, from lunch or recess). He was cool, and I am really grateful to him for introducing me to all those books!

Another teacher, Mr. Gardner also made a huge impression on me. He was my math teacher. He was very dapper. He often wore a bowtie. I think I saw him at the US Post Office, when I started to work there, in 1963. In Mr. Gardner's classes, I excelled in math, with grades well within the 90-percentile range.

In 1957, while at Gladstone, I was entered into the Science Fair, at Crane High School. My project was explaining how a radio works. Today, my youngest daughter teaches at Crane. And, of course, my career has always been involved with Electronics and Radio, since Grammar School (beginning with classes at Julius Hays Elementary, then, Tilden Tech H. S., the Air Force, colleges, etc., etc.)

Milton was my best friend, at Gladstone. He and I used to go to the Public Library over on Madison Street, east of Damen Ave.

He excelled in athletics. He was a jock, and a scholar. He had many trophies, in Track and Field, and in other sports.

At Gladstone, Milton, others, and I continued to be engaged in the customary boxing, and fighting. But, I got into an actual fight, and wrestling match, one day. During this fight, I was swung over, my forehead banged into the concrete sidewalk, and a huge swelling formed on one side of my forehead. This cooled me down some, for a while. During this time, we lived at 1729 W. Washburn. There, I really enjoyed playing softball, and "Alley Ball." Gee and I played hours and hours of basketball, east of our house, in the alley, where we would hang a makeshift hoop, and go to it!

Once, our class went on a Field Trip to Douglas Park. I think we had all experienced puberty by then. And it was really interesting and enjoyable to physically flirt, and interact with some of the girls at this time. Some of my schoolmates seemed surprised to find out that I was not just Nerdy (intellectual), but also sensual. Youthful indiscretions, folks! We were not as old, and presumably mature, as Arnold Schwarzenegger was, when he did his groping.

At the age of 12, I had a newspaper route on the West Side, and I delivered newspapers (at times) from about Racine Avenue to past Damen Avenue, near Roosevelt Road. I also maintained the house while my Mom worked. And I cooked full meals, and learned to use cook- books.

During the time when we lived on Washburn is significant to me because I lived a very balanced, disciplined, and productive life. I was a jock! I was a scholar! I was involved in work, play, music, singing, dance, and sports. I was socially popular, and involved in many pursuits.

When I was 12 or 13, I bought my own bike, and I commuted to my Newspaper Route office, on Racine, from as far away as Christiana Ave.

We moved farther west, and then I went to Julius Hays Hess Upper Grade Center. I had Warner Saunders for a Spelling teacher. Yes, *the* Warner Saunders, of NBC, Chicago. I was in Gifted classes. My homeroom teacher was Mrs. Jollie. My teachers were all great! I was something like a Valedictorian at Graduation. I made a speech to the class, visitors, parents, and dignitaries. And I excelled in just about all my classes, though some of my wood and metal shops were not always all that easy. Hess did a lot of testing, and I scored at high levels in just about all areas. Verbally, I scored very high! Duh! Some may have actually been at college level! (If that is possible.)

Aunt Annie Mae bought me a black, silk (or blended) suit, but I wore a rented Tuxedo to the formal graduation. I was very handsome!

During this time, in 1957 or 1958, Fred came back from Indianapolis, where he had been living, with Fred Senior. He had been sent there because boys in Chicago had tried to recruit him into their gang(s), in about 1956. Fred started to help Robert Washington clean his store, after hours, at 1311 S. Christiana Ave.

Later, I helped Fred. Then Fred worked at Kopper Kettle; and I cleaned up the store by myself. I mopped the floor, and stored away the produce, and some of the fruit, and covered over other items. During this time, we lived a few doors south of Washington's store.

9

OK. I want to tell you about another girl. Her name was Annie Gary, and she lived down the street, just a few houses south of Washington's Christiana store. The Douglas Library was just to the west of the store, on Thirteenth Street.

Annie, maybe it was Anne, was always so perfectly groomed, dressed, and beautiful! One day, I remember seeing her, hair blowing in the wind, looking fabulous, gorgeous, and divinely beautiful! And these impressions will never fade away!

Anyway, beautiful women sometimes take your breath away! Annie took my breath away many times! But, Annie was taken! Her boyfriend was an older guy. I think he was an amateur, or semi-professional boxer. Of course, Annie used to come into Washington's store. But, she used to always have one of her brothers with her. Beyoncé Knowles reminds me of her.

One more word about the library: I spent a lot of time at Douglas Library, researching, reading, studying, thinking, watching people. I love libraries. (There, I read a lot about the Planning Commission of Chicago). I love books!

1.3 Summary of Events From Age 14-17:

So, at the age of 14, I began working in Washington's Grocery Store. First, I would just clean up and mop the floor, after store hours. Later, I did all the jobs at the store. And I bought all my own clothes, and also helped provide money for our family.

At 15 and 16 years old, I continued working at the grocery store, and I provided the money for my High School needs, including commuting to and from school, (on Chicago's South Side), and class, band, and ROTC uniform fees.

During the time when I was 11-16, I was an excellent student. I was an Honor Student, and I read newspapers and magazines to stay informed on all events worth knowing about in the world. I also read books about politics, religion, and current events. At the age of 15-16, I was in ROTC, the High School Band, and I was on the Wrestling Team.

At the age of 17, I was so eager to be 18 that I tried to put my age up to 18. At 17-18, I bought my own brand new car, and I bought two "lots" of land in Hawaii.

1960:

I worked more and more in Washington's store. In about 1960, he got another store, on 5th Ave, and Karlov, and then he got another building complex, and some stores, on Pulaski, just north of Jackson Blvd. I helped Mr. Washington set up the latter two grocery stores. He had made me responsible for ordering his weekly supplies of canned and boxed supplies (inventory), on Christiana - sometimes at one of the other stores.

And I was in-charge of maintaining an inventory of produce, poultry, fresh meats, and fruit. I remember when we first started selling Money Orders, on Karlov. We were then State-of-the-Art, High Tech, in 1961! Mr. Washington introduced me to the Philadelphia Enquirer, the Wall Street Journal, and other newspapers. And he introduced me to Positive Thinking advocates, like Napoleon Hill, and others. He let me use his records by Napoleon Hill, and other advocates. I read Muhammad Speaks. I read about Islam, and about Muslims. Beginning then, I read just about all the African and African American authors. I also read Keats, Shelley, Sandburg, (Yes!), Edgar Allen Poe, and others.

I am forever grateful to Mr. Robert Washington for giving me the opportunity to develop my abilities, talents, and skills. And Mr. Washington was/is an excellent African American role model, now, and forever!

In about 1961, I had a fistfight with a guy who came into the store, giving me a hard time. His name was Shorty. And I don't remember how the situation escalated. But we ended up outside, on the north side of the store. Of course, I kicked his butt! I beat on him! And this kind of reminds me of that boy in Mississippi, William. Remember, I was then on the Wrestling Team, in excellent condition, about 16 years, old. So, I just beat on him, popping him on the head and body. But he kept coming back for more. I don't remember how this ridiculous incident ended.

When I started Tilden Tech, H. S., in 1959, I had Honors Classes. I joined the band, ROTC. I joined the Wrestling Team. I worked. And I traveled to school via CTA Bus, from near Christiana Ave., and Roosevelt Road, to 47 St., and Union Ave.

I did really well, except for a class in Geometry, in about 1961, where the teacher read out the problems, instead of giving out written problems. I created a system of coordination with another good student, and we would review the problems, by phone, as necessary. And this took care of that obstacle, after early difficulty.

In about 1957, I remember really hearing jazz, for the very first time! I listened to a saxophonist, and he blew me away! And I listened to Gene Ammons, Sonny Stitt, Cannonball Adderley, Miles Davis, and Nancy

Wilson! They all blew me away! They still blow me away!

I went to see Gene Ammons and Sonny Stitt, here in Chicago, with a very gorgeous young lady named Sherry. Sherry lived across the street from Washington's Grocery, on Fifth Avenue and Karlov. Subsequently, years later, I saw Miles Davis, in person, with Gloria. Miles is awesome!

In about 1961, I had a class about all the important legal cases in the history of the republic. We read, studied, and analyzed the cases. This course blew my mind! It still blows my mind! I mean, I was so excited and impressed by the legal arguments, and the legalistic process. I got very angry over the cases involving slavery. But the legal process was, and still is very compelling to me; and I am still very interested in legal matters, and important legal cases.

At Tilden, my Band Director was John Olivo, and he was a great influence in my life. He gave me private Clarinet lessons, and in return, I did some work, at his house, in the southern part of Chicago. Playing in a band is a wonderful experience. I learned about classical music. I became a First Chair Clarinetist. And we visited other schools, or places, during band contest periods. And we played at some ROTC functions.

During the summer of 1961, I went to Summer School, at Hyde Park High School. I experienced working under a different Band Director, a wonderful experience.

In about 1961, Muhammad Ali was up and coming! He would predict the round when he would put his opponent down! We loved Ali! He had the killer instinct! He was a proud warrior, taking no prisoners, sort of like me! He was one of us!

In 1962, I got sick, in about late September, or October. I also had my school band instrument, a clarinet, stolen. I got way behind.

I decided to withdraw for that school term. I continued to work at Washington's Grocery. I bought my own brand new car. I bought land in Hawaii. And I bought furniture for our house.

Of course, I remember when President Kennedy was shot, in the fall of 1962. I also remember thinking that I would like to become president, and my brother, James, would be my Attorney General - just like the Kennedy's!

In 1963, I went back to school, to a private school, Britannica Academy, and got my High School Diploma. In 1964, I started college, at Loop City College.

When I was about seventeen, I remember thinking that I wanted to have four wives, at the same time - one Caucasian, one African, one Asian, and maybe one Native American. In my heart, I was a Muslim. I mention this here, because men are always after the women, because of that irresistible attraction that women have. Their eyes, mouth, and face look different from the man. And the structure of their bodies is so different from the man's! And so are their walk, voices, personality, and other characteristics. Most men are just flabbergasted and dumbfounded to hear about men being attracted to men, or women being attracted to women.

We think women are an awesome creation! And we Muslims just love children, especially our own! They are so wonderful, so interesting. I have enjoyed having my three children sometimes sleep on my chest. They love it! And it is so delightful to hold them when they are 0-7 years old. You even enjoy changing their diapers. Their appearance on earth changes you, to fit in with their arrival!

When they start walking, it breaks your heart to see them fall! But they finally get it, and then they follow you around, wherever you go! Often, I would like to have dozens and dozens of children! At least a hundred.

I don't know if what the Bible says about Jacob, and his four wives, Rachel, Leah, Zilpah, and Bilhah is true or not, but it seems probable. Anyway, Prophet Muhammad, who is the reincarnation of Moses, had 9 wives. But, he thereafter, decreed only 4. He learned his lesson! Seriously, I want the reader to understand that men used to sometimes set up marriages to create alliances among peoples, groups, and nations. It reduced the likelihood of war and conflict between peoples, groups, and nations. So, Muhammad had nine wives.

In about 1961, I met Rosa Walls, from Alabama. (I think that is her last name.) She was Seventh Day Adventist. And I met a lot of her girlfriends, and associates. I met her family, the Wallace's, living in Maywood, Illinois. Rosa was quite gorgeous, intelligent, and attractive. Culturally, intellectually, physically, this is the type of woman that was quite attractive to me, as a lifelong mate.

In about October, 1963, I started working at the Main Post Office, on Van Buren St., in Chicago. Later, I also worked at the O'Hare Post Office, and I worked at the Franklin Park Post Office.

I met Haki Mahubuti, (then, Don Lee), at the Post Office, in 1963. Haki encouraged me to read, though I was already reading just about everything I could get my hands on. We continued to correspond, when I went into the Air Force. Haki's company, Third World Press, co- published my first book, in 1978.

I heard Haki at a lecture, in 1996, in Oak Park. I think he spoke about his father, named Jimmie Lee! Haki did not like his father's name. Ooops! That's my name, Shorty!

Haki is a dear brother, and one of my role models, because of his discipline, and his productivity. But many, many African Americans are much too fair (and intelligent) to be calling themselves a color, and one which they absolutely are not! And why does any person identify himself or herself with a color, anyway? A person is NOT a color. A person, a real, developed, mature person is much, much more than his physical appearance. I have a separate article and argument, called, "I Call Myself African American," which see, in this book.

In the early 60's, I visited the Muslim Mosque, on Greenwood. I saw Malcolm X in person! I went to several of Mr. Muhammad's conventions. I often saw Malcolm on Kup's show, on Channel 11. We adored Malcolm! We still do! Once I saw and touched his vehicle, at Malcolm X College, and I felt like I was touching something holy, something sacred!

We always admired and respected Dr. King. But we just adore Malcolm! He is one of us! We are "Nationalists," Pan Africanists, Pan Islamists, and we are warriors! We don't take crap from nobody! And we will try to kill you if you screw around with us!

Mr. Hammurabi was another great influence on me. I used to visit his lectures, (on the Southside), buy his books, calendars, artifacts, and newsletters. He had gorgeous stories about Africa and Africans, and about his travels in Africa. He would have movies, films, and sometimes guest speakers.

In 1965, I was going to college full time. Then, I dropped one or more classes, because of the classes, and/or work. I was concerned about The Draft. So, I talked to my Air Force Recruiter, and I joined up.

On May 10, 1965, I joined the US Air Force, and I went to Lackland AFB, in Texas, for Basic Training. After Basic Training, I went to Kessler AFB, Mississippi, for Tech School Training, in Electronics Intercept. When the Air Force became aware that I am Muslim, after about 21 weeks of schooling, I was switched to Air Traffic Control, and assigned to Grand Forks AFB, North Dakota. Grand Forks AFB was a Strategic Air Command, or SAC Base.

In Tech School, at Kessler AFB, I did well in my Electronics classes, and again, my grades were well within the 90-percentile range, reinforcing my confidence in my intellectual abilities. Generally, the "smarter" individuals went into the Air Force, not the Army. Many of my class-mates were quite proficient in class. I don't remember anyone being dropped from class, after about the fifthteenth week. I think someone may have been dropped earlier on.

At Kessler AFB, I often hung out with some of the numerous student visitors from African countries. They were from all over: Ethiopia, Somalia,

14

Nigeria, Cameroon, etc. I met Joseph Aloga, from Kano, Nigeria there. He introduced me to some of his sisters, very lovely, beautiful women. I still have some of their photos; and I have Joseph's photo.

I enjoyed my job as an Air Traffic Controller/Dispatcher. I dispatched for aircraft and helicopters.

It would become more hectic and demanding around the tower when high-ranking officers were departing or arriving. Otherwise, pilots were engaged in routine training flights. It was just about like any civilian job, except the pay was less. After a few months, I moved into a Trailer Home, which sometimes had one other occupant. And frankly, I had a good life!

Once, when I still lived in the barracks, I prepared to fight a room-mate, a Caucasian guy. I always do a physical exercise routine, basically what I learned when I was on the Wrestling Team at Tilden Tech High School. And I used to be pretty good with my fists! I went through my routine more strenuously for a few days, and I felt ready to kick his a....!

The fight never took place! And we became more respectful and cordial toward each other. I have no idea what prompted my preparations for a fight! I do remember, he was not the cleanest. He would dump cologne on himself without actually taking a shower. He was about my size, at the time, 5'10" and 150 pounds.

A group of guys, and me, sometimes went to Winnipeg, Canada, on weekends. We would drive up there, go to a few parties, and drive home. Some guys had wives or girlfriends up there. Sometimes, we would go to Minneapolis, Minnesota. The only times I recall visiting the town of Grand Forks, was to go to college classes.

I voluntarily signed up to go to Korea. Then, in the late summer of 1966, Fred Robinson, Sr. died. I started the paperwork to get a Hardship Discharge, to return home, and to assist my family.

I recall that I returned to the Post Office, in 1966. I got an official Discharge from The Air Force, effective, January, 1967.

Enroute to Grand Forks, I passed through Chicago. And I met my future wife, Gloria Campbell, in December, 1965. We met again when I came home in the summer of 1966. We corresponded, while I was away at Grand Forks AFB.

Gloria was young, lovely, and sexy! She was also funny, and a Chicago down-home girl. I remember seeing her once, on a bus, going to work at a Department Store, on Madison Street, near Pulaski Road. She looked so beautiful, so gorgeous!

Once a man, (we thought) made a disparaging remark about her, or us.

I was ready to kill him, with a hammer, or a crowbar! I got my weapon, and walked back past where this guy was sitting, in a garage on Eighteenth Street, between Harding Avenue and Pulaski Road, going west. Then, I

walked back past him again, going east. I think he recognized me. I
didn't get a peep out of him! Yes, I was very young, very young!

Gloria and I were married February 15, the day after Valentine's Day,
1967. First we had a son, Jimmy Jr., born 7/22/68. He died of bronchial
pneumonia, after about two months. Then, we had Tonya, in 1970, and
Runako, in 1972.

In 1968, I left the Post Office, and got a job in Electronics, at
Telemotive, a Division of Dynascan. I was *the* production, maintenance, and
repair department for Radio Remote Controlled Transmitters, which
operate Overhead Cranes, at auto, steel, warehouse, and other facilities.

In 1969, I went to work for AT& T Western Electric, at Cicero and
Cermak Rd., in Cicero, Illinois. In 1972, I went to work for AT& T Long
Lines, at 311 W. Washington Street, Chicago.

At Western Electric, I became a Lead Man in the analysis,
programming, and testing of Electronic Switching Systems (ESS),
specifically, switching, memory, and control circuits and frames. At Long
Lines, I maintained and operated K and L-Carrier, and Radio Routes, and
video feeds. I also worked in Radio Engineering, and Planning Engineering,
and I engineered several line-of sight radio routes. I performed Prior-
Coordination Engineering of proposed Radio Routes. In Planning
Engineering, (I) we planned radio or cable facilities for Indiana, and parts of
Ohio and Kentucky.

When I returned home from the Air Force, I went back to college,
part time. And I continued to work for the Post Office, first it was full
time. Later, it was during some part of the year, like Christmas.

On June 11, 1969, we moved into our two-flat building, at 5312 W.
Adams St. In about 1971, my brother, James, started living there, in
one apartment. And my Mom lived in another.

In 1971, I helped Ruwa Chiri (of Zimbabwe), and others
incorporate United Africans For One Motherland, International,
(UFOMI), a Pan African organization.

In the spring of 1971, I studied for and got my First Class FCC
Radio Operator's License. At AT&T Long Lines, it was necessary to
have this license to work in Radio.

In the summer of 1971, I started practicing Yoga, and I took some
formal classes in Downtown Chicago.

In 1971, I helped the African American Students Union, at Wright
City College, produce a Talent Show.

Here, I want to mention an excellent mentor, facilitator, and role
model at Wright City College, in 1971: an African American, Dean
Timuel Black.

In about 1970, before my brother, James, moved into the apartment on the second floor, I was concerned about an unruly tenant. I borrowed Fred's gun, and I was ready to use it on him! And I borrowed Fred's or Mom's gun, in about 1971, just in case, when there was a dispute involving a passenger that I used to take to and from Wright City College. And I say this to make the point that my family does not take crap from anyone! And we will be prepared to kill you!

Now, I am law abiding, peaceful, extremely generous, kind, and humanitarian. If all people were like me, there would be no need for a Police Department, maybe anything like the hospitals we have today. But, the following entry will begin to make the point that we have a lot of injustice, corruption, and lawlessness in this country, among the powers that be. And we need to have radical change in this country, in the legal system, in the political system, in the educational system, in the social system, and in the THINKING!

Beginning, in 1994, I have seen the lying, corrupt, degenerate, lawless thugs in the judicial system of Illinois, and at DCFS, and in the political system of Illinois. We have the documentation. We know who they are! And we will get them sooner or later, one way or the other, some way, somehow!

In about 1971, I took a Business Law course at Loop City College. I love the field of law. I love to hear the arguments, and the logical, rational building up of, and development of the arguments. But corrupt, immoral lawyers, and corrupt judges and Public Defenders really make my blood boil!

In 1975, I helped Hannibal's Shule Ya Watoto School, located on the West Side of Chicago, produce a Fashion Show, at Malcolm X College.

In 1975, I was promoted into a management level job at AT&T Long Lines.

In the spring of 1977, Gloria and I officially obtained a divorce. I kept the children.

In about 1978, or 1979, I visited Runako's school, DePriest Elementary School, when she made a presentation about Malcolm X. And **I had the strange feeling that ALL the children there, dozens and dozens, *were my children! This made a huge impression on me. Still does!***

In the fall of 1978, I published my first book, *People Of The Future/ Day.*

In about 1978, the Pope, John Paul II came to Chicago, and I, among thousands, saw him in Grant Park. It was partly cloudy, but the sun shone through, in places. I remember, there were clouds all around, but there was an opening, and it seemed that the sun shined down *directly on me*, where I was sitting! That experience was/is still very strange to me! Earlier in the day, I had been practicing "bringing up the clouds!"

Round about this time, and to about 1980, I used to experiment with bringing up clouds, like my Native American ancestors do, and I would watch this process take place from the top floor lounge, at 10 South Canal, Street, Chicago, on the weekend, or after regular work hours. I'd practice like this: I'd bring up the clouds! Then, let them subside. Then, bring them up again! (I need to see if I can still do that!)

On June 15, 1979, I incorporated African Kongress, International, (AKI), a Pan African organization.

In 1979 and 1980, AKI sponsored a Fashion-Dinner-Dance, to showcase itself and to raise money.

In 1980, I was on the PAC, funded by the Johnson's (in cosmetics and automobiles, respectively), with then Senator Harold Washington, Dr. Bobby Wright, Alderman Clifford Kelly, and others, which set the stage for Harold to later run for Mayor of Chicago.

In about 1979, I learned that the USA is known in Scripture as Babylon, The Great, Head of the Seventh and the Eighth World Empires, or Powers. The Seventh World Power includes the USA, UK, Canada, and Australia. The Eighth includes the Seventh, plus NATO, and the European Union. I have watched that allegation for over 25 years. And I have seen an awesome, awesome vision confirming the same, in about 2001-2002. It is a renewal of Greece and Rome, the Fifth and Sixth World Empires. It is a monster. And God is not very happy with it!

On July 20, 1980, I obtained yoga, Spiritual Unity, consciously, for the first time, in this lifetime. And there were many outward and inner manifestations or reflections of this.

I want the reader to understand a few things about Yoga. In a semi-sleep, or sleep state, we sometimes routinely have out-of-body experiences. We Astral travel! We have awesome visions! We see amazing things, in visions. In meditation, we can have DIRECT experiences with what we call God! I call some of this, Time-traveling! *We are "conscious" while asleep, our "senses" extended!*

Sometimes, my experiences were so amazing that I would get up the following morning, and be just a little surprised to look in the mirror and see that my appearance had not changed overnight. **In visions, I have raised the dead, briefly visited the Holy of Holies, seen God, Allah; seen angels, and visited the most beautiful and joy evoking places!**

One of my goals, one of my aspirations, in the 1970's was to become a saint! No kidding! And frankly, I think that naïve desire reflects who I am. And I believe that I have wronged no man or woman, in this life. I always try to amend for transgressions that I make, sins of commission, or omission. Sometimes people try to take advantage of my generosity and my kindness.

My son once said he thought I was a "softie." I think they said the same about Jefferson. Said it was out of character for him to wrong anyone. There are many, many other experiences and realizations I've had regarding my belief that I am the reincarnation of him.

One thing struck me in about 1999, when I started reading his autobiography, which I downloaded and printed from the Internet. It was his prolific use of the symbolic "and," (&), just like I used to do, in this lifetime. See "People of the Future/Day."

There is the other characteristic in me, that of the warrior, with the killer instinct. Well, just let me say that I have been a ruthless warrior in some past lives. I have seen this, and regretted it some, but I do accept the total me, and the different aspects of my personality and character.

In 1983, I purchased a house in University Park, Illinois. And my daughters and I moved there on 10/21/1983.

In 1984, I went to work for Allis-Chalmers, in Matteson, Illinois, as a Compiler. And I was The Coordinator of Provisioning for Instruction, Repair, Parts, and Maintenance Manuals for Electric, Diesel, and Gas Fork Lifts, responsible for *all* government related, foreign, and other contract procurements. I (we) made the manuals, and the accompanying software that accompanied all Fork Lift trucks.

In 1988, Tonya went away to college. In about 1991, Runako left home, for college.

In 1989, I received an AAS Degree from DeVry Electronics College, in Chicago. Our (my) Senior Project was to design, install, and operate a Yagi Antenna. I am still interested and intrigued by the function of antennas. In 1989, I went to work for Motorola Corp., first in Northbrook, then, in Arlington Heights, Illinois. At Motorola, I analyzed and tested Mobile Phones, for the Japanese, USA, and European markets.

In 1990, I had an automobile accident. It just damaged our car. Runako was with me, and my reaction was, "What are they trying to do to me?"

Since then, I have learned: In this lifetime, God wants me to go to my sub-conscious, come to Him, and to learn, and to write.

And I think He will set up a Theocracy, and we will live in Him, and in Christ. But I think that Christ is that force within the sub-conscious. If we live at all, after the judgment, we will live in him. Quite frankly, **I have seen "Christ" as "tracks,' or a pathway, in several meditations, or visions.**

And this reminds me of the Tsunami that hit Indonesia, on December 26, 2004. My first reaction was this: I said (to God), "How could you?' "How could you?" I was upset to see the children, women, and men being taken out like that!

Then, I became more thoughtful. He brings us here! He takes us out! God brings souls into the earth, and He can, and does take us out, whenever He wants to. Maybe, many of the souls have gone on to better places. God brings us here, and He takes us out! And when He's ready to take us out, He'll find a way, to take us out!

In 1992, I left Motorola, and started writing more, and doing Electronics Contract work.

In 1992, I produced another book, initially a play, and several books were spun off from it.

In 1994, Noah Patrick was born to *Kathy Bishton* and I, for my Pseudonym is Youssef Khalim (Joseph Khalim), for "God shall add a son."

Also, remember what I said earlier about Catherine Bishop? Katherine Bishton developed a disability when she had an incident similar to Christopher Reeve's accident, of being thrown from a horse, and injuring his spine. Her accident happened in the gym, though. So, in a sense, *Katherine Bishton* is similar to Catherine Bishop. There is, of course, more to this. But my point is to show you an example of how patterns may continue throughout one's life. We used to get *eggs* from Catherine. God gave us an egg from Katherine to nourish us spiritually. He gave (my heart), Noah!

In about 1996, I remember going to Ottawa, Illinois, in connection with trying to prosecute a legal case against criminals that work at DCFS. And I remember feeling a sense of entering holy and sacred ground, in the vicinity of Ottawa, and upon going up the steps, and into the Court House.

In 1996, I moved back to the Chicago urban area, first to Oak Park, and then to Chicago proper.

In about 1996, I had a dream about having a red Beretta, an automobile, in a dream, or vision. And I have understood the meaning to refer to the Beretta of the Cardinal, i.e., relating to my rank in The Church.

Beginning in about 1996, I revived my previous publishing company. And I incorporated a second organization.

In July, 2000, I started work for A large Telecommunications company in Bridgeview, Illinois. Here, I maintain, grow, and protect our Mobile Phone Network, in the Chicago Market. I also perform Acceptance Test

Procedures, which include verifying construction of Mobile Sites, loading and programming them, and bringing them on the air.

From 1992, to the present, I have continued to write, and to record many amazing revelations, visions, dreams, and insights. Are these experiences not recorded in this, and the other sixteen or so books?

On 8/4/1999, I had the awesome experiences, visions, and meditation sessions that indicate that I am the reincarnation of Thomas Jefferson! And, the details? Are they not in my previous books, especially *The Resurrection of Noah*?

On 2/23/2002, I had the awesome experience, vision, and meditation session that indicates that Thomas Jefferson was/is the reincarnation of Jacob, the father of the famous 12 boys. And, the details? Are they not in my previous books, especially *The Resurrection of Noah*?

On 5/2/2000, I had the awesome experience, vision, and meditation session that indicates that Prophet Muhammad is the reincarnation of Moses! And, the details? Are they not in my previous books, especially *The Resurrection of Noah*?

Today, 2/19/2005, I am working on finishing this, my fourteenth book, "The Second Coming."

21

2 AUTOBIOGRAPHICAL - GOALS PAPER

On 1/27/95, I produced an Autobiographical Goals Paper, for Governors State College. It is an interesting shorthand biography of me, from 1944 to about 1995. And it is interesting to see what my views were in 1995, considering the venue (college course), and the requirements. See below.

James Lee Robinson   1/27/1995

I was born in 1944, the 3rd of six children, in Cleveland, Mississippi. I was born into a Southern Baptist tradition where the values that society now talks about were actually practiced. Every able-bodied person contributed their time and skills toward providing the requirements of the household.

Parents were respected. Elders were respected. Church attendance was taken seriously. We children were expected to know the Sunday School Lessons, and we were expected to stand up and explain what those moral lessons meant to us.

I grew up primarily (until the age of 11) in an almost classically rural, Mississippi, farming environment. Most of what we needed of food came directly from the land. Some clothing was made. Often, the fuel, wood/coal, for heat or cooking was secured directly by us.

My southern experience has made me mindful of just about every area of life because we lived in a kind of self-sustaining community where just about all of our needs were taken care of through our efforts and the abundance of nature.

My family immigrated to Chicago in 1955, when I was 11 years old, and that's when my significant formal education began. I did well in school, and even made up some time missed in Mississippi by getting some "doubles." I skipped some grades.

After graduating High School in 1964, I attended City College, (part time), in Chicago.

I joined the Air Force in May, 1965. I certainly did not want to be drafted by the Army. I went to formal school in electronics, but was shifted to Air Traffic Control, Dispatcher.

In the Air Force, I continued with my education about organization, planning, teamwork, communication, and coordination.

I added to what I had learned in ROTC. I added to my understanding about motivation, drive, physical, and psychological functioning.

I further learned about bureaucracy, research, documentation. I used some of these skills to get an early discharge from the Air Force when my father died.

Earlier, in 1964, I became a Muslim. But I just, essentially, added Islam onto my Baptist beliefs. I felt that Islam had something to do with my being transferred from electronics (in The Air Force). I learned about peoples' fears and prejudices.

Anyway, just as I blended Islam with my Judeo-Christian tradition, I added some non-contradictory aspects of Eastern tradition. I began practicing Yoga in 1971. The practice of Yoga also increased my awareness and concern about the interaction of mind, body, soul, health, vitality, biology, genetics (morality, harmony in nature, truth, Our Creator, etc.).

In 1968, I left the Post Office (to get into electronics), and I became *the* Transmitter Dept. at Telemotive. I furthered my understanding about running a department. I learned about quality control, and I learned how to set up a repair or production area. (Telemotive was located in Chicago.)

When my son died, I learned about loss and grief. I learned about death. I learned about love. I learned about the ignorance of know-it-all youth.

Later, I had two daughters born to me. And they have taught me lots of things. They let me see myself, or their mother (in them). I see my father, especially, in one. They taught me about role models. They taught me about "Do as I say, not as I do."

As I attended their ballet, or piano lessons I learned about moral support or financial support. I think I have learned a lot about how we can create a better society - or better people. My children inspire me.

I have owned property for all of the time since 1969, except for about 1 year. This has made me more aware of business practice and the application of good business management techniques.

Also, at AT&T, I attended various classes in Labor Management Relations, Psychology, and management styles. I have always used the opportunity to write, in business. So, anything is fair game, including minutes, reports, or memos.

I also have an abiding interest in history, politics, and social science. I have been involved in creating two activist organizations.

I desire higher degrees because I need the credentials to validate my wide and deep understanding in just about all areas. In fact, the areas where I need expertise are more easily listed, and include computer science, (facility with higher mathematics), physics, and chemistry.

23

BOARD OF GOVERNORS BACHELOR OF ARTS
DEGREE PROGRAM

GOVERNORS STATE UNIVERSITY

CHRONOLOGICAL REC0RD

James Robinson

6/3/44	Birth date; Cleveland, Miss.
10/64	Graduated Britannica High School, Chicago, Ill.
Fall, 1964	Embraced Islam.
January, 1965	Attended City College, Chicago.
May, 1965	Enlisted in The U.S. Air Force.
January, 1967	Received Air Force Discharge.
January, 1967	Ended Leave-of Absence from U.S. Post Office.
February, 1967	Married, in Chicago, Ill.
May, 1968	Employed with Telemotive, Division of Dynascan, Chicago.
July, 1968	Son born; died September, 1968.
June, 1969	Purchased two-flat building, in Chicago.
10/69	Employed AT&T Western Electric in Cicero, Ill.
April, 1970	Birth of daughter, in Chicago.
Spring, 1971	Obtained FCC Radio Telephone Operator's License.
Spring, 1971	Began Yoga practice.
September, 1971	Attended City College, Chicago.
May, 1972	Birth of 2nd daughter, in Chicago.
June, 1972	Employed with AT&T Long Lines, Chicago.
Spring, 1973	Grandmother died.
Summer, 1975	Produced Fashion Show at Malcolm X Col.
4/77	Obtained Divorce; retained custody of daughters.
October, 1978	Wrote and Published a Book of Poetry.
July, 1980	Filed legal Complaint against major corp.
October, 1983	Purchased house in University Park, Ill.
August, 1984	Employed with Allis-Chalmers, Matteson, Ill.
September, 1987	Attended DeVry College, Chicago.
May, 1989	Employed at Motorola Corp., Arl. Hts., Ill.
May, 1992	Completed manuscript for "This World Is Mine," a play.

24

1992-1993	Wrote several essays, on economics, religion, and philosophy.
February, 1994	Continued poetry writing.
March 17, 1994	Birth of son.
January, 1995	Began legal Complaint against major corp.

3 BLESSINGS TO LOVED ONES

Blessed are you, Ruby (*red*), mother of Jacob, and blessed is the fruit of your womb: The Sons of God, The Sons of Men, Princes of Egypt and Israel, and Princes of the United States of America!

Blessed are you, Ruby, mother of James and James, and the wife of James (Jimmy), blessed are you among women, and blessed is the fruit of your womb, for this multiplicity of James' is a sign unto you, to take note and understand, for James is a variation of Jacob, and one is Jacob, the renown twin, father of the 12 Tribes, and the same is the *redhead,* Thomas, for Thomas *means* twin, and the surname is Jefferson, which means, "The Son of God," and he is the son of Samuel, which means "His name is God; the name of God, and God hath heard." And so, you are in a sense The Mother of Zion, Queen of the Nile, the mother of Mighty Men of old, Moses, Joshua, the Kings of Israel, the Queens of Egypt, mighty men of the New World, and the Resurrection. Hold on to what you have, for the time of the Harvest is nigh!

Blessed are you, Ruby, mother of Jefferson resurrected, the one with the red birthmark, the nickname, Red, and blessed is the fruit of your womb: men of renown, those who sat on the thrones of Egypt and Israel, the honored Children of God.

And blessed are you, Samuel, the father of Jimmy. For, you are much loved and adored, an Urban Legend, a genius, inventor, musician, electrician, carpenter-builder, manager, mechanic, and admired for your wonderful mind!

And blessed are you, Noah, and Tonya, and Runako. You are much loved, admired, and adored! And blessed are you, Gloria, the mother of the Children of God.

And blessed are you, Thomas Jefferson, red-man, the Son of God, the Renaissance Man, for you took the 12 votes of the African Americans to succeed as king, (as president), making them heirs to the promise, and citizens of the USA. And, what they earned, was bought, for a price.

And blessed are you, Sally Hemming, mother of those who move with uncertain, secret, or unknown heritage, in the new World. You will receive your blessing, for your father and mother are blessed. And you will receive your reward. For, God has said, "The children of Jacob shall become as numerous as the sands of the sea. And if you can count the sands of the sea, then you can count the children of Jacob." You are not alone!

Blessed are you, Sally Hemming, de-facto wife of Jefferson, and blessed are you among women, for your day will come. You are Queen of Europe, and Queen of Africa, the likeness of Vanessa Williams, Miss USA; Blessings and honors to your children thereof, the Sons and Daughters of God.

And blessed are you, Noah, among the Sons of God. You are a blessing, much loved and adored, appearing to your father as a beautiful, red fox, and confirming the heritage of the Sauk, The Fox, and The Meshwaki, "The People of Red Earth," and a reminder that Adam was a "Man of Red Earth," as were The Kings of Egypt, indigenous folk of the world.

Blessed are you Noah Patrick, the son of James, the son of Samuel, for you were longed for, sought after, and pursued. You are The Six of Diamonds. You too have a wonderful voice! May the Kingdom of God be strengthened in you, in the earth, among The Chosen, and in the 144,000, as it is in Heaven! You were conceived on National Flag Day, and born on St. Patrick's Day. And this is a sign to you, that you are very, very special, and much adored, among The Sons of God, and The Sons of Man. Relax, be still, and possess your rightful heritage.

Blessed are you Tonya Tracy, the Daughter of Jimmy and Gloria, the Daughter of Samuel. You are The Ace of Diamonds, and perfect in matter, in material things, and the one with The Golden Voice. You were the apple of their eye, that wonderful child. How delightful to be your parent! You are very special, so says The Lord of Creation, so says our God. Be perfect now - just as you were perfect then!

And blessed are you, Runako Soyini, the Daughter of Jimmy and Gloria, the Daughter of Samuel. You are The Four of Diamonds. Though, as Jimmy Jr., you were The Ace of Diamonds, like Tonya. You too have a wonderful voice. You are very special, Doubly Blessed, and the Daughter of a Prince, for sure. You are the Resurrection of Jimmy Jr., out of love and forgiveness, proof of God's Mercy and Grace!

For has not God said, in the Holy Qur'an?:

39:42 It is Allâh Who takes away the souls at the time of their death, and those that die not during their sleep. He keeps those souls for which He has ordained death and sends the rest for a term appointed. Verily, in this are signs for a people who think deeply.

And 6:60 says: It is He, Who takes your souls by night (when you are asleep), and has knowledge of all that you have done by day, then he raises (wakes) you up again that a term appointed (your life period) be fulfilled, then in the end unto Him will be your return. Then He will inform you what you used to do.

27

In Chapter 2:28, it says, How can you disbelieve in Allah? Seeing that you were dead and He gave you life. Then He will give you death, then again will bring you to life, and then unto Him you will return."

And blessed are you, Dorothy and Bobbie, the beautiful Daughters of Ruby, The Daughters of Zion, Daughters of the Nile. Blessed are you among women, and blessed is the fruit of your womb. Much blessings and honors to you and yours, forever and ever more!

And blessed are you, The Daughters of Annie, the Daughters of Zion: Princess Bessie, Princess Hattie, Princess Leana, Princess Ruby, and Princess Annie, the lovely Daughters of God! Blessed are you among women, forever, and ever more!

And blessings, and honor, and glory to the Daughters of Jacob, the Daughters of Zion, Queens of Africa and Europe, like Sally Hemming, the beautiful, admired, and loved - the Daughters of our Father, Abraham: those of the curiosity and interest, and those of The Future/Day, first, to Lizzie Shinault, and Katie Shinault, and to Annie Watson (Big Mama), and to Ruby Watson, the Honorable Mother of James, a Son of God, a Son of Man, and to Rosa Walls (of Alabama and Chicago), to Sherry, and to Gloria Campbell, the Mother of Tonya and Runako, the wife of James; to Dorothy and Bobbie, the Daughters of Ruby, to Juanita Gillespie, the Daughter of Samuel, and to Elma Robinson, Melovee Schoffner, Alma Jenkins, Marsha Ward, Audrey Bennett, Lorraine Scott, Anita Branch, Melody Knight, Anne Barber, Cathy Costner, Brenda Washington, Dorothy Malone, Tanisha Love, Kathy Bishton, (the Mother of Noah), Kathy Rodriquez, Jean Cox, Menai Edwards, Tamara, Beverly Shannon, and Gwendolyn Brooks, (Poet Laureate of Illinois), and to the Daughters of the Heritage, Time-travelers, and those who move between the races, cultures, and genders.

Blessed are you, Gayle, Lori, Alina, Alla, Teresa, Lara, Monika, Margaret, Ekaterina, Natalia, Svetlana (s), and Galina, and all those of the likeness of Sally Hemming: those with whom interactions with demonstrate the magical, powerful, and divine relationships between a man and a woman.

Blessed are you, James and Jimmy. Your symbol is 722, or 227. You are that Bright and Morning Star, the Ace of Spades! And very special, so says our Lord, our God! You are Robinson and Green, the son of Samuel, the Servant of God, and you are a songbird for our Father, God! Some of your African roots are in "Middletown, Nigeria." And you are very, very African, from the times of the beginning, in the very distant antiquity. You are Jacob, Jefferson, James, Jimmy, the father of mankind, father of the United States of America, father of Judaism, Christianity, and Islam, and father of the Church; ample evidence that no man should be called a minority.

Praise and blessings, to the Servants of God, The Sons and Daughters of God, the Messengers of Allah, to Moses, who is also The Prophet Muhammad, and to Joshua, and Samuel, the founders of our Church; to Isaac and Jacob, our Patriarchs, and to Abraham, our Father, and to Jesus, the Son of Mary, the Messiah, our Most Honored Servant of God, who joined with God, to end our previous rituals and sacrifices; and to Daniel, and to John, the Baptist, (who is Elijah) and to John, The Beloved; And to our Prophets of the New World, to Thomas Jefferson, Martin Luther King Jr., Malcolm X, and others. May God, our Lord, bless and bless you, forever and ever more!

Praise and Honor to our Lord, God! There is no God, but God: Master of the Universe, He who sits on the throne alone, "with hair like wool, as white as snow." He is The Ancient of Days, our Mighty, Mighty God! Praises, and honor to our God, forever and ever, and ever, and ever, forever and ever more!

For God created all that there is. There is no God, but God! Amen.

4 THE FAMILY AND I

Note: After I finished the previous segment of my autobiography, Runako said it was boring! She said I should add more sex and violence! She was trying to be funny, of course! But, what the heck! I added more sex, violence, and detail, below!

4.1 My Own Intelligence

I feel very confident about my own abilities, to learn, to understand, and to apply information on just about any topic, including Science, Mathematics, Physics, Psychology, Astronomy, Biology, Electronics, Tele-communications, History, Literature, Music, Internet, Publishing, Business, etc. My only desire would be to absorb information more quickly and efficiently, and to be able to present it in a clear, concise, effective, and efficient manner.

I used to read through swaths of the Encyclopedias, and/or the dictionary. I used to record, and playback to myself college vocabularies, over and over, year after year. I also once used the Verbal Advantage vocabulary system. I think a person's actions, ideas, and words reflect his or her deep-seated awareness of, and concept of self.

Sometimes, because I am quite imaginative, creative, intuitive, insightful, knowledgeable, educated, persistent, and flexible, I feel that I can hold my own with anybody on the planet, in almost any discipline. I readily admit that I am not nearly as efficient as some; I don't absorb information as rapidly as some, but many people scan over information, without getting down into it. And many, if not most people seem shallow to me.

OK, I am a legend in my own mind! LOL!

Cases in point: Why would "intelligent" people call themselves "Black," or minority? Why do they call themselves "kid," the devil's advocate, white? Why do people strongly identify with a nation? God doesn't care about your nationality!

Why do most politicians have very little integrity? Why don't people examine life, examine themselves, and be true to themselves, and their mission in life?

Why do people, human beings, tolerate and consume the garbage distributed by TV, Cable TV, radio, and many other outlets?

Why don't the so-called intelligent and educated people know that the USA is head of the Seventh and Eighth World Empire, called Babylon, The Great, in Revelation?

Why would about 58 million-plus people vote for a person remotely like George W. Bush, and his corrupt, lying, satanic administration?

Why do people carry on as if this country's history, and trend, will continue indefinitely? Whatever has a beginning is likely to have an end.

Why do some people say that homosexuality is normal? How could it possibly be "normal," when carried to its logical implementation, there would be no reproduction, and mankind would just die out? Is conduct which creates the absence of life normal? And clearly, The Bible and The Qur'an say it is an abomination and an aberration.

Why do African peoples allow the conditions in Haiti to exist? Why do some people betray their own family, or ethnic group? How can you explain a Condoleezza Rice or Colin Powell? Why do they work for the devil (George W. Bush, and his administration)?

How can anybody look about the universe, at our Solar System, the earth, the natural world, and at civilizations, cultures, and life, and say God does not exist - when the foregoing is contrary evidence?

4.2 Exemplary Orators

Over the years I have marveled at some of our very good orators: Rev. Jesse Jackson, Sr., Rev. Al Sharpton, President Bill Clinton and Hillary Clinton, Dr. Joseph Lowry (formerly of SCLC), Dr. Martin Luther King Jr., Malcom X, President John F. Kennedy, Senator John Kerry, Vice President Al Gore, President Barack Obama, and Senator Ted Kennedy. Isn't it amazing and marvelous how they do that!

4.3 I Was An Agnostic?

When I was about 18 or 19 years old, I went through a stage where I called myself an Agnostic. As I have mentioned elsewhere, I read Shelley, Keats, Jean Paul Sartre, Camus, Fanon, George Padimore, and many others, including the Marxists-Leninists. They only take logic and reason to a certain point. Then, *they* become irrational! They can't answer the *ultimate* questions. See *Healing Begins With The Mind*, by Youssef Khalim.

4.4 Audrey And Us, In University Park

In 1984 Tonya, Runako, Audrey Bennett, and I went to see Niki Giovanni, at Governor's State University, in University Park - just like we did a number of things together, as a group.

Niki's performance was entertaining. Seems like we met her onstage, after her performance.

One time, we "explored" together: We trekked across the fields and forested area behind (west of) our house at 1044 Blackhawk Drive, all the way over to West Hamilton Road: a distance of over half a mile. We walked through woods, bending and navigating under and around hanging tree limbs and branches, pushing or pulling them out of the way. We crossed over little streams and creeks, across a field, and navigated our way down little trails made by animals; and finally we arrived on Hamilton Road!

We routinely saw herds of deer or just a few, maybe one or two deer in back of our house. I would sometimes tape them on a video camera we purchased from Sears, in Forest Park, in about 1986. We bought the video camera when Tonya worked at Sears, and we got a discount through her employment status. But you know what? We paid about

$1000 for that camera, and today, almost 20 years later, you could buy three camcorders for $1000, with features and performance far superior to that camera of 1986.

Once Audrey, Tonya, and Runako all tried to wrestle me, in our living room, in 1984. I won, but they gave me a run for my money! Runako was particularly aggressive! Little brat!

This is how I did it: I would take one of them and hold her down on the other two. And I would hold onto a wrist of one or even two, at a time. See, in wrestling they taught us, first, how to take down the opponent. In practice, you learn how to scoot down beside or under an opponent. In one practice routine, you spin 180% on your head, first lifting, then, replanting your feet! We learned how to use the opponent's weight against him!

We learned how to never let the opponent keep you in one place. Keep moving, spinning, twisting! Know how to use leverage and your weight against your opponent. These are things you never forget, and you learn to do much of this instinctively!

Once in about 1989, Runako and I went to see my most honored Queen: my Dream Girl, Gwendolyn Brooks, at Prairie State College, in Chicago Heights, Illinois. I took notes of that session. I still have them. From memory, I think the session was on some aspect of how to use creativity and imagination, and improve our writing skills. Gwendolyn was/is a saint, sent down here to be a role model for humanity, and to help us find our way back "home."

In about 1988, Tonya visited DeVry University, in Chicago, at 3300 North Campbell Avenue, where I was going to school. She also graduated from High School that year. She was listed in Who's Who among High Schoolers. She won many, many awards while she was in either Grade School or High School.

These awards were in many areas: academics, singing, scholarship, and even a Beauty Pageant Contest. We used to keep her awards and Runako's on top of the piano, in University Park. And we have photos, even some video of some of those awards, as they then appeared.

4.5 Tonya, Back in The Day

Anyway, Tonya probably visited DeVry a *few* times, but I'm not sure of exactly why some happened. Tonya was always my Right Hand, almost from the time she could walk. She followed me around. We went almost everywhere together. We used to go to meetings, seminars, Book Reviews (At Lou Palmer's Bookshelf). And we used to go to Haki Madhubuti's Third World Press, on south Cottage Grove Avenue, or to Kwanzaa celebrations. Tonya and I used to go to the Adler Planetarium (on the lakefront, over by Meigs Field) frequently, from the time she was maybe four or five years old.

I remember that Tonya, Runako, and I had a problem when we tried to take Runako in with us once. Runako was too young to enter the Planetarium on that occasion.

Once or twice Tonya helped me with paper work at a House Ware and Sales company where I was working, in about 1987, before I started attending DeVry.

In the summer of 1989, she worked alongside me, and also on her own separate shift, at Motorola Corporation, in Northbrook, Illinois.

Tonya was very family oriented, and focused her energies, time, and resources on our family: herself, Runako, and me. She helped organize, document, and manage our various necessities, including clothing, food, financial matters, or just keeping the house conditions operational, adequate, and orderly; cleaning, washing, vacuuming, shoveling snow, sometimes even cutting the grass.

We would keep a list of things that needed to be done. I called it my "Agenda." We would try to prioritize items on the list. Then, we would just cross off items as we completed them.

She and Runako used to have certain social or financial school obligations. They had performances that involved going out of town, for example. They had Field Trips, weekly piano lessons, costume requirements, etc.

When she left and went away to college, our family, and many aspects of our lives became like the title of the book by the African Writer, Chinua Achebe, *Things Fall Apart*. Things fell apart! But part of that was due to the financial demands of college. Unless things change in the way we do things, we should always plan very carefully for college.

Back at DeVry, I was in The Video Club. We used to tape certain events, some using my own video camera. We would prepare and edit the event in the Cable Public Access Studio in University Park, and play the video on the TV station at DeVry. And this would be seen on various TV monitors at the school.

At DeVry, I was ahead of many of my colleagues in Boolean Algebra, for example. I had studied some of that stuff for years. I was also somewhat apart in the area of writing. After all, I had been doing some of that for years too!

Our senior project, or thesis, involved the development, construction, and installation of a Yagi Antenna, for broadcasting. I think one or more of Tonya's visits to DeVry involved the Yagi Antenna, and/or the Video Club.

Tonya was the First Born in some ways. We lost Jimmy Jr. after he was with us for less than two months. Doctors said he died of Bronchial Pneumonia. So, we were so delighted and happy to bring Tonya into the world in April of 1970!

And she did not disappoint! What a delightful child! Very energetic, very happy, ebullient, smiling, laughing, running, playing: that was Tonya!

In 1968, we bought a brand new Plymouth Barracuda, *which cost about $2900*! That's right! Now, auto prices are just about **10 TIMES THAT MUCH!** That's because our monetary and economic system is based on a Currency (not money). An unfair, unjust, discriminatory, racist, corrupt Currency System is like a runaway train or virus - destined to destroy itself and kill its host.

In 1969, I left Telemotive, Division of Dynascan, and started working for AT&T Western Electric, at Cermak and Cicero, in Cicero, Illinois. Gloria used to take me to work, and pick me up after work. And, of course, she brought Tonya along. Somehow, Tonya used to often be in the back window of that Barracuda when I got off work, about 10:30 or 11:00 PM. Gloria would park on the north side of Cermak Road, over by the Hot Dog and Italian Beef Fast foods Restaurant. That place used to have really good Italian Beef sandwiches! And sometimes we would get ourselves this treat! Then, we'd go home!

Once, at home on Adams Street, Tonya was goofing around in the pantry. A really heavy cabinet fell over on her, but she held it up, with her hands, until we rescued her, as if she was a 25-year-old guy! I think Tonya was about four or five years old then.

As I mentioned elsewhere, I sometimes used to sleep with all my three children on my chest (not at one time, you Dingbat!) It just always seemed like a natural thing to do. All my children are spoiled brats!

I remember doing my vocabulary readings on tape, just after Runako was born, before she and Gloria came home from the hospital. Tonya would take the microphone and say, "Where's Momma, Jimmy? Where's Momma? She gone get the baby! She gone get the baby!" Then, she would blow into the mike, making noisy sounds with her mouth. We may still have that tape. I think we last played it in the eighties - and laughed!

Tonya used to go with me, and follow me, almost everywhere. If I was working around the house, she was there, maybe handing me some tools. If I went to the hardware store, she was there! I remember once when she was about 4, we went to the hardware store on Madison Street, between Laramie and Lockwood, on the south side of the street.

Tonya winked her eye at this man we saw in the store! At the time, she said she "inked" her eye at him! LOL! She was a flirt at 4, "inking" her eye at a man!

Both Tonya and Runako went to Pre-School at Shule Ya Watoto (It means School For Children, in Swahili). They put on a dance and musical performance at the end of the school term. Shule Ya Watoto was a great experience for our whole family. Finally, the school put on a Fashion Show and Musical/Dance performance at Malcolm X College, located on I290 and Damen Avenue.

Another parent, Nabii and I, effectively produced that show! It was a lot of work, including helping with the management and coordination of ticket sales, getting backdrops for the models, selecting music and sound equipment, coordinating the hiring of entertainers, helping to manage the models, printing up flyers, promoting and advertising our show, etc.

Then, Tonya started school at DePriest Elementary School, by Adams Street and Central Avenue. She excelled! Then, she went to a Magnet School, much further north! Finally, she went to Michelle Clark, near Laramie and I290.

After that we moved to University Park, Illinois. And she went to Deer Creek Junior High, and finally Crete-Monee High School. As I said elsewhere, she was always exemplary, and she is listed in Who's Who Among High Schoolers of her time.

Tonya graduated from Howard University, in D.C., and she is now a manager at large national corporation.

4.6 Runako

I am over 80% sure that Runako is the reincarnation of Jimmy Jr.! But I did not know this until about April of 2004. I saw this in a convincing vision!

I (we) petitioned, and mourned, and repented so after the death of Jimmy Jr., that The Lord, our God, took mercy on me, (and us), and He (with Runako's assent, I'm sure), sent her butt right back down here to be with us in May of 1972!

She was the quiet baby. She, unlike Tonya wanted to sleep a lot! So we let her sleep.

Runako was a good to excellent student in school also. But she used to sometimes get in trouble for being a social gadfly. She talked a lot!

Runako and Tonya performed a lot of dance and singing in Grade School, High School, and college. Runako has done film work (movies), and she has traveled over much of the USA, and Western Europe, performing.

When I wrote this passage, Runako was a teacher at Crane High School, in Chicago, where I did a Science Fair, presenting on how a "radio" works, when I was 12 years old! When Runako used to talk so much in school, it was because she was practicing and rehearsing for her profession as a talker - a teacher! Now, she is a Counselor at another high school.

You want to know more about Runako? Was Runako, in her essence, not captured in the poem of the same name, *Runako*, in 1978? Please see that selection, in *People Of The Future/Day!*

And yes, Runako, you are the daughter of a Prince or king, because you are a Princess!

4.7 I Am A Yogi

Here I need to give you some background. As you know, I practice Yoga. And on about 7/20/1980, I attained full unity, and this coincided with actual, real and amazing, tangible events here in Chicago. (There is no such thing as an accident, or a coincidence. There is action/reaction, cause/effect and cycles in nature. We are just not always aware of the specific causes of effects that occur).

In Yoga, we strive for unity through physical regimes, breathing exercises, and through **right thinking, and right actions.**

I have seen visions of what occurs, symbolizing unity for me. I have merged into the sun, went right into it! And this experience has been very joyful, full of love and ecstasy. And immediately following this event in the visions, there has been soft rain, a little more than drizzle. And there is a kind of choral music that follows. It is as if Heaven itself, and the universe celebrated/celebrates my unity (with God)!

On 7/20/1980 my concomitant spiritual unity was met with tremendous rains and flooding in Chicago, and surrounding the house where we lived. An enormous amount of tree limbs were hurdled to the ground on our, and the nearby streets! The streets and avenues flooded, basements flooded! Some people went into the streets to try to unclog drains, so the water could go down into them. My neighbor, one house east of ours, did this!

Our basement flooded! The water was climbing up the basement stairs. There was nothing we could do. We threw our own little party! I know this sounds bizarre! But we sang and danced, up- stairs, on the first floor. Tonya played on her portable organ. We sang Christmas carols! That's what Tonya played. And later we played Stevie Wonder's *Songs In The Key Of Life*, on our record player, and we sang along!

At one time, I danced with Tonya in one arm, and Runako in the other. Tonya was 10, Runako, eight! Now that really seems nutty, but at the time, it seemed so very appropriate! I believe we just felt compelled to celebrate my unity, with nature, with God! That incident always reminds me of Anthony Quinn, dancing on the beach, in *Zorba, The Greek!*

4.8 I Began to Seal My Destiny

On 7/21/1980, I gave a Safety Presentation, fresh off my Yoga Unity of 7/20, the previous day. It had spiritual references in it. It caused a stir! The second level manager above me got involved.

Now, I will tell you this about me. When I am in an argument, debate, or confrontation, *and I think I am right*, I will never, ever back down! I would rather die first!

So, I did not back down in our back and forth, with Stanley Bushhouse. So, Stan and others asked me to take a day or two off while they sorted through the matter. Later that week, my immediate Supervisor, Frank Dadosky said AT&T wanted me to take a test. They wanted me to take a Psychological test. I consented. I took the test. It showed me to be superior in my functioning!

AT&T and their fake Psychologists, and a fake Psychiatrist, Benjamin Blackman and others started withholding parts of the test results, and lying about other parts.

I sued AT&T. But first, I went through the EEOC Complaint process. I kicked their butt in court over, and over. It was just me, after my cowardly, ignorant attorney dropped off the case, very early on. On October 6, 1983, AT&T cut me a check for $85,000.00 to settle the case!

I tried to put a curse on AT&T! I feel very, very Native American sometimes, when I do my Yoga, and my breathing exercises. We identify with the Meshwaki, also called the "Fox" Native Americans, now living in Tama, Iowa, "The People of Red Earth!" I do the chants, the dances, I get into the rhythm, and the whole ambience of being Native American becomes a part of me: in my mind, personality, and character. Sometimes, I even do the physical aspects, but not in public view.

So, I tried to put a curse on them for their lying, corruption, and cheating! I went through the whole dance routine, and the mental, and emotional process to put a curse on AT&T! AT&T was busted up in 1983 for violating antitrust laws!

Today, on 4/3/2005, AT&T no longer exists! However, on 1/13/2006, AT&T has reconstituted itself. Even institutions never die, but just take on a new form! (Like Reincarnation!)

(And what became of Alexander Hamilton and Aaron Burr – these two who crossed me? And what became of Laban (who tried to defraud me, the father of Leah and Rachel)?

And of the details of this case, are they not in the Federal and Civil Courts, here in Cook County, Illinois?

Now, as a result of this confrontation with AT&T, I really delved deep into the fields of Psychology and Psychiatry. I had already taken Psychology, in 1966, at Grand Forks, when I was in the Air Force. And I had read and studied several other books on Psychology.

Now, a person's psychological functioning does not change appreciably, unless there are huge changes in their life – and they cannot adjust and cope with the changes. My life, even I, changed very gradually over the years. And my psychological functioning has remained constant over the years: EXCELLENT. And I am very grateful for the opportunity that the incident with AT&T afforded me to really learn about Psychology and Psychiatry!

Below is a copy of the results of the Psychological tests of 1980. The tests ALWAYS come out just about EXACTLY identical.

The following includes my Psychological Profile and other personality indices, characteristics, and traits, taken from *Healing Begins With The Mind*, by Youssef Khalim.

5 PSYCHOLOGICAL OBSERVATIONS OF THE AUTHOR (VARIOUS)

Content- consists of various personality inventories- or self-analysis

Subject- is the father of Noah.

As mentioned in the observations of Noah, (concerning his parentage), his father was recognized as being "gifted" in his formative years. And he was also an Honors Student in High School. He has been called very talented because of his writings.

5.1 The MMPI And Other Indices

This data speaks for itself, and the language, terms, and descriptions are taken wholly from the MMPI two volume set. The comment on the "L" validity scale is instructive. It is a T score of 56. It says these "values are likely in test subjects who are ministers, reformers, social activists, or evangelical missionaries." I was "called" to the "ministry" on 9-27-94. The F scale is a 50, and the description "indicates conformity and would indicate few deviant beliefs, attitudes, or unusual experiences, and show a tendency to avoid endorsement of socially unacceptable, threatening, or disturbing content among the test items." My comment would be that is essentially true. But there are some possible important differences with the materialist psychologists, and their fellow travelers. We believe that dreams and/or visions can be "normal" and useful.

We believe in, and know something about "God," as should be the case with all normal human beings. *We believe in the dreams of Jacob, in the dreams of Joseph. We believe in the visions of Daniel, for instance; and we believe in the visions of John, the - Beloved.* From experience, I have a certain sense of the reliability of my own dreams, or visions. And I also know that my own dreams and visions are in conformity with those of our ancestors- that I have just mentioned. And we know that our whole Judeo-Christian-Islamic Tradition, and its real adherents believe essentially I as do. I also say that if the materialists were normal, they also would have dreams or visions, and they would better understand the nature of man.

And since they are not normal, they must be dysfunctional, and abnormal. And since they don't know anything about God, and he's everywhere; again, the materialists must be abnormal. But I will tell you (if we can try to use an analogy), God is more like the weather. And you cannot stop summer, and you cannot stop winter- when it wants to come. You can only adjust to it, and you can study it. And even if you want to study the weather, you better have some respect. And you should realize that God is very much higher than the weather. Again, God is like the Quarterback and the *front four* of the 1985, Chicago Bears.

He will give you the ball. And He will block for you. And you should stay right there "in His back pocket." And you shouldn't try to get ahead of God. For, He will surely block for you. And, when He gives you that ball, you hold it in tight against your body to protect it. And you stay in that back pocket until you see some daylight. And then you run, like Walter Payton!

And you run over, around, or through anyone (or anything) that gets in your way! And you don't stop until the arms go up, and the cheers go deafening! And everybody breaks all out in smiles: "Touch down!"

Or, God is like the jab of Muhammad Ali. And he goes rat-a-tat-tat against the nose of devils! And God has even been known to do an "Ali Shuffle" at times. And when the devils get distracted with the jab, or the Ali Shuffle, good people must knock the hell out of them!

Or, on the other hand, good people should keep a stiff left jab in the devils' face, so that when the devils get distracted, God hits them with a Mike Tyson like uppercut and an overhand right, and knocks the hell out of them! So, you really shouldn't mess around with God! And when people choose God, and choose to do his work, (and to do the right things), and they become God's Chosen, you really should be careful about messing around with them!

And, yes, God is love, and grace, and all of those qualities too. But there comes a time to cut bait. And it is now time to cut bait, to create a world where those qualities will abound in those that are left around. The others will be cut off! And "We" will give them what they have earned!

One of the other problems we have with those materialists is that they lack moral content, or direction. And they do not immediately notice (and state) that an individual opposed to Nazi Germany because of its racism, and inhumanity is not necessarily disordered. The direction of the ruling classes is psychotic!

And if someone in the former Soviet Union is opposed to its materialism, then, he may be healthy, because that society was disordered. And if good people do not, now, stand up, in the USA, and overthrow this materialistic, irrational, destructive, and evil economic, and social order; then they are not healthy.

And if they are intelligent enough to be aware of the disorder here, and have a conscience (and do not stand up for this positive change) – they will probably acquire symptoms of disorder. And the first thing that we must do in that process of affecting change is to rely on, and call upon our God to make the right changes. Then, we will legislate JUBILEE, and other rational, moral precepts listed in "Jubilee Worldwide!" which, see. And the USA will become a place that God (Himself), will be proud of!

On another matter, there is going to be some controversy. But again our guide is our own experience, and our religious documentation: Matthew 11:14 says, "And this I will tell you, if you will make room in your minds, that he is that Elias whose coming was prophesied," in speaking about John, the Baptist. Matthew 17:10 repeats this perspective. So does the Qur'an, but it is done in a different manner. Anyway, I believe in "resurrection," or reincarnation. And this only means that the soul is immortal, minds semi- permanent, and bodies perishable. See the "Resurrection of Noah" for a fuller explanation.

In conclusion, this still makes the validity scales valid. All the remaining material is some true, some partly true, and some not true, in the descriptions.

5.2 Myers-Briggs Type Indicator

This description is essentially true. I would only add that I am significantly introverted, and strongly intuitive. I am also very much the thinking type. But because of my also outgoing nature, it may not be immediately apparent that I am strongly introverted.

5.3 Whole Brain Dominance

The individual here possesses Whole Brain Dominance. This means he uses a lot of creativity and imagination. Then, he is very, very thinking, (rational, logical), so he can organize these concepts, or ideas.

It has been observed that the subject here is very fixed, and this is partly true. In some ways, he is very adaptable, very flexible. Much of that is innate. It is like part of the DNA. And much of this has been studied and analyzed in a process where we look at energies. We look at where the power centers are. We look at predispositions. And we correlate this with traditional psychology and other disciplines. We look at how this is used in every day experience. But again, we see things in an affirmative, positive way. "Fixed" may be seen by us also as relentless, solid, stable, consistent, persevering, constant, indomitable, determined, convinced, unwavering, immovable, eternal, etc.

In fact, we see the so-called psychologists' excessive use of negatives, like overcompensate, overachieve, underachieve, etc. as evidence of the fact that the formulators of such terms are, themselves, morbid, negative, and unhealthy. Furthermore, we see this ignorant and faulty attempt to "judge" God's creation as morally wrong and evil. And this may be further evidence that they have been studying rats and other animals too much, and trying to remake man in that image. The better perspective to use regarding human beings is that they will often "Do whatever is necessary to affect a certain outcome." This is because they are made in the image of God, and (should) have creativity, imagination, and reasoning.

One of the things that psychology will learn: people can and do attain balance, harmony, and even maturity within a certain personality type. This would be like a rose maturing and blooming as it has been predisposed, and a lily doing likewise in its domain. And so it is ignorant, even evil to speak of deficits in speaking of either when they don't become each other. Don't try to make a rose a lily, or vise-versa. A rose is very content to be a rose. In other words, a writer may have traits that incline him to develop certain skills that would be different from those of a, say, Michael Jordan. And then, the basketball player, Michael, may not quite have the traits to be a star baseball player.

Also, bigger is not necessarily better. Psychologists speak in terms of "gifted" people being larger than others as if it were a positive (in itself). If bigger were better, then the Tutsi of Burundi should be the masters, or superiors of us all. And where would it leave the Asians, who are generally smaller in stature than Westerners?

Consider a Black Hole. It is one of the most powerful forces in the universe. Even light cannot escape its gravitational strength. So, it is concentrated energy. Likewise, human beings (or other objects) may have beauty, intelligence, charisma, logic, grace, poise, strength, speed, argument, a sense of justice, etc. that just holds us spellbound. So, there are many qualities that are attractive, and powerful. And

42

these don't necessarily depend on size - unless you are a Neanderthal Materialist.

We will bet on King David, over Goliath, any day! And in the Mississippi Delta (where I come from), we were taught, "The bigger they are, the harder they fall!" So, look at the force and power of the individual. What we find is that people choose a body that will be most effective in doing whatever is sought in a particular lifetime. Even if you are "too" beautiful, it may be a hindrance in a particular environment. And it may distract energies, or efforts from what may be more desirable. And a Mahatma Gandhi (e.g.), will not come into manifestation in the USA, in 1965, (looking like he did in India), and hope to lead the USA very far. Big, (LBJ- Lyndon Baines Johnson) was the choice.

And a person who dislikes Americans, for instance, might come here (into manifestation) looking like the all-American hero! And you will not suspect the traitor, until he does his evil deed! So, he was just hiding out in the most unsuspecting body available- and waiting for his opportunity. And you will find many Americans like that. For, that is why America is now in such sad conditions. So, again, this "bigger is better" is one of the ignorant, materialist, pseudoscientific notions that will fall by the wayside. Also with respect to those supposed "gifted" or genius types (and somebody has tested, or ascertained this status) -Why aren't they aware and doing some- thing about changing this society into a just, equitable, and rational society? Could there be something wrong with the tests?

When psychology becomes a real science, it will know:

-Free will is a birthright (right) given to souls throughout the universe. So, they have the right of choosing.
-The purpose of (human) life is for growth, maintenance, and development.
-Souls choose (decide) when, where, and in what human form they will resurrect in. i.e., they decide what ethnic group, nation, community, family, etc., they are to resurrect in.
-Souls choose an environment to resurrect in which is compatible with their level of development, goals, aspirations, needs, wants, and purposes for a particular lifetime. It is more true that souls choose parents, than the other way around. Parents can only invite. Souls choose. Part of the lesson here is that even though a soul may have the DNA of the parents, he may choose to be opposed to the values

43

and ideology of those parents- because his purposes in that lifetime are in opposition to the purposes of the parents.

- Souls become what they are. i.e., just like a kernel of corn grows into a healthy or weak stalk of corn (it will not, e.g., turn into a tomato); a "good" soul will usually find a way to grow into a "good" and virtuous person. Of course, the reverse also holds true. A scholar will become scholarly. A scum bag will become what he is, even though he is CEO of a Fortune 500 company - or a priest. The manifestation will reflect the environment. I.E., Robin Hood is still an honorable person, though labeled an "outlaw." Malcolm X, even with a criminal record, is honorable.

-The presence of certain kinds, or levels of "intelligence" may actually interfere with the usage of the God-link (which we call Christ) because *choices* made by that individual are in opposition to the "Christ" principles (of sharing, caring, justice, courage). An example of this may be the sociopath, the psychopathic personality, cowards, the selfish, etc.

-Many events that happen to individuals are really "blessings in disguise." When I got hay fever, at the age of 22, I turned to Yoga. And this helped create the experiences and state of mind to perform my mission in this life. When FDR got polio, he learned perseverance, courage, a fighting spirit, and empathy for those with problems and difficulties. Look at King David. Look at JFK (and his back injury). Look at Martin Luther King Jr. *Again, if the psychologists want to learn something about people, the first thing that they must learn is that people are all children of God, and they will often do whatever it takes to affect a certain outcome.*

5.4 Introduction to Dreams and Visions

-Dreams reflect past or future conditions. Whenever dreams meet the "present," they end. Dreams can be "organized" for greater clarity (or realistic, vivid, reflection) by one being more truthful (especially to oneself), and living a more healthy, productive life; and for example, practicing meditation.

-"Visions" in healthy individuals are levels of experience sometime during the sleep state, but may be more possible when the mind and body have attained a certain amount of rest, or relaxation. Unlike dreams, where sometimes one knows that he is dreaming, in

"visions," one is (then and there) conscious of the experience of the vision.

Depending on the state of the individual, visions may contain high levels of energy.

The subject matter of visions here, just like conscious experiences, cover a wide spectrum. They may involve objects, people, events, or places. And they may involve taking part in activities.

When there is greater energy, there is usually greater clarity and/or understanding of what lesson(s) are to be learned. But, many experiences here, just like in the conscious experience, have apparent limited usefulness. And like dreams, visions seem to only reflect past, or future "events." Visions seem to be a more direct interaction with what we would call spiritual forces, because, even though in a kind of sleep state, we are "conscious." And there is always the presence of moving energies. The prophets have generally described these as "winds," or seeming moving "flames," etc.

-Dreams and visions are a reminder that we are all like our Father, God. For, we were made in His image. He is Omniscient, Omnipotent and Omnipresent. He is time. He is timeless. We live and have our "being" in Him. We are part of Him. If we are righteous, in dreams or visions, we experience wondrous things. We can learn things that have escaped our conscious notice. We can have confirmation of beliefs. We can see the *possibility* of "future" events.

5.5 Time, Space, And God

These aspects are more fully dealt with in the section, "What's On Your Mind?" which, see.

In closing, the evolutionary level of individuals will be reflected by heredity, and their environment. But souls have chosen environments and DNA options (bodies) that correspond to what they are, and what they want, or need to accomplish in a particular lifetime.

There is much that is useful in psychology and psychiatry. But much of the theories and ideas are like those of someone partially color blind, and just entering puberty, but deciding what imagery, love and life are all about. Freud, Jung, and Adler are examples. Freud contributed much, but even Jung and Adler were more advanced in many ways. Jung may have been the more advanced.

45

But Jung, himself, was not whole (or integrated within himself). And that is why he did so poorly in finding real solutions, or getting a full understanding. So, the "mind sciences" need to become focused- and grow up.

We should recognize that while left, or right brain dominance may be useful for concentration, or rigorous specialization- they probably don't (can't see the big picture).

And we must start with the basics. I have discussed these in "What's On Your Mind?" And we must approach the study of God's creations with proper respect- which is not the case, now. The motivations must be correct!

Then, I believe that "good," healthy, normal people, with normal, or above intelligence, with "whole brain dominance" (possibly, the "Mother of All Brains"), and "O Positive blood (possibly, the Mother of All Blood), and Unity within themselves can find better solutions to whatever problems we have-because the DNA might be "better."

I believe people with Unity can often use skill beyond the intellect, or what we call insight, or intuition (in a conscious, or dream state). It seems to be a more direct interaction with what we call the Christ- link. And, when it is the higher mind, it is the truth- or God. It will make perfect sense. It will be rational, logical, just, beautiful, obvious. So, we should locate, and make maximum use of people who have these qualities.

Finally, it should be noted that the author has practiced a variation of yoga, since 1971, and this has affected the quality (clarity) of his dreams, and/or visions. Prospects? We shall see.

5.6 Healthy Psychological Inventories (An Example, Using Test Results From the MMPI)

5.7 Indices of Psychology

   1. Number of scales with T score over 70 —none

   2. Number of scales between T score of 40 and 60—8 of 13

   3. Disturbance Index (DsI)—461.78, where 550 and above is used to determine significant degrees of disturbance are present. 549 and below are called normal adjustment.

   a. L – 0   j. Pt - 2.7
   b. F – (-25.2)   k. Sc - 3.6
   c. K – 178   l. Ma - 49.8
   d. Hs - 0   m. Si - 4.7
   e. D – 43   n. A - 2.38
   f. Hy - 17.8   o. R - 0
   g. Pd - 69.6   p. Es - 37.4
   h. Mf - 42.4   _____

   i. Pa - 35.6   DsI - 461.78

   4. Mt (maladjustment) Raw score is 2, T score is 34.12

   5. SOC (social adjustment) Raw score is 2, T score is 36.

   6. Index of psychopathology ((Ip) on a scale of 1 to 10, it is 3.5 (Ip = .1Pa+ .06Sc- 6.26=3.5).

   7. Indices in Leary's interpersonal diagnostic system.

   a. DOM (dominance) is 2 (i.e., DOM vs. submissiveness)
   b. LOV (love) is 39 (i.e. love vs. hate).

8. Other Indices

   a. AI (anxiety index) is 42.66
   b. A (anxiety, first factor) is 35
   c. At (Iowa manifest anxiety) is 34.72
   d. R (repression (repression, second factor) is 53

e. Repression, factor scale II is 43
f. IR (internalization ratio) is .863
g. HOS (manifest hostility) is 37
h. Hostility, Finney, is 35.43
i. Hostility, McDougall, is 33.81.
j. REL (religious fundamentalism) is 49.
k. PSY (psychoticism) is 45.
l. PHO (phobias) is 35.
m. Autocratic (power) is 21 (i.e., leader vs. follower).
n. DEP (depression) is 38.
o. K is 68
p. ES (ego strength) is 67.

9. Validity Scales

L - 56 (moderate elevation). Elevated scale values are likely in test subjects who
are ministers, reformers, social activists, or evangelical missionaries.

F - 50 (middle range). This indicates conformity and would indicate few deviant beliefs, attitudes, or unusual experiences and shows a tendency to avoid endorsement of socially unacceptable, threatening or disturbing test items.

K - 68 (moderately elevated). A low K is associated with the psychotic tetrad (scales
2, 4, 6, 8). A high K is associated with the neurotic triad (scales 2, 3, 4). Scorer in
high average (57-64) is well adjusted, self-reliant, and easily capable of dealing with everyday problems.

There seems to be few emotional disturbances or threats to self-esteem or self-control and little interpersonal wrangling. These persons show restraint, prudence, and circumspection in their everyday conduct and behavior. Also:

reasonable	ingenious
clear thinking	enthusiastic
showing initiative	verbal
readily ego-involved	sociable
enterprising	being a good mixer
resourceful	taking an ascendant role
versatile	

48

having wide interests and fluent
having high intellectual ability

These men were competent, effective, and well balanced. There is no implication that they were not concerned about their own personal or social status, rather they are quite content with the way they find themselves.

Moderately elevated scores (65-74) indicated efforts to maintain an appearance of adequacy, control, and effectiveness.

10. Basic Scales

a. Scale #1 is 49, low (Hs) Hypochondrias

Friends described men as having narrow interests and the women as being well balanced and conventional. Adjectives typifying were:

alert	argumentative
quick to adjust	intelligent
at ease in oral expression	outgoing
cheerful	having initiative
capable	persuasive
good-looking	competitive
responsible	warm

The general picture seems to be one of freedom from hampering, neurotic inhibitions, from over evaluation of oneself and one's own problems, and from undue concern about adverse reactions of others. These persons are also characterized by an energetic and spontaneous

pursuit of the goals and aims in which they have a sincere interest and investment. In the self-reports of the men, only the descriptions sensitive, emotional, and soft hearted appeared in the analysis.

b. Scale #2 is 44, low (D) Depression

Lower scores reflect a naturalness, buoyancy, and freedom of thought and action that lead to easy social relations, confidence in taking on tasks and effectiveness in a variety of activities. The lack of inhibition in low 2's may, in certain contexts lead to negative reactions from others, however, as a result of hurt feelings, slighted friend-ships, and threatened confidences. Men are seen by their peers as balanced, self-controlled, self-confident. Also:

active	good natured	adventurous
hardheaded	affected	humorous
aggressive	impulsive	alert
informal	autocratic	intelligent
cheerful	outgoing	egotistical
outspoken	emotional	quick
energetic	responsible	enthusiastic
restless	excitable	self-seeking
generous	prone to show off	spontaneous
witty	talkative	having initiative

c. Scale #3 is 62, high (Hy) Hysteria

The adjectives describing the males were:

fair minded	energetic	persevering
enthusiastic	prone to worry	assertive
enterprising	socially forward	alert
adventurous	generous	affectionate
mature	sentimental	clear thinking
cooperative	talkative	good tempered
kind	grateful	individualistic
verbal	mix well socially	courageous
have wide interests		

Judges rated high males:

clever	inhibited	enterprising
enthusiastic	spunky	imaginative
infantile	impatient	thankless

both responsible and irresponsible
independent in judgment
high degree intellective ability   ability to think for themselves

The psychological picture is one of social participation and easy accessibility, ready involvement in activities, and participation in social activities.

d. Scale #4 is 58, high (Pd) Psychopathic Deviate

These persons are adventurous and courageous, sociable in both senses of the word (socially forward and mixing well), talkative and verbal, enthusiastic, good tempered, frank, generous, fair minded, and individualistic. Also, said to have wide interests and like drinking. They are characterized as sensitive and prone to worry. They are described by their peers as hostile and aggressive in their interpersonal relationships, sarcastic and cynical, as well as ostentatious and exhibitionistic. IPAR assessed this type as tense, moody, nervous, and resentful, aggressive, immature, irritable, leisurely, and unemotional.

e. Scale #5 is 61, high (Mf) Masculinity-femininity

These persons were characterized by their peers as sensitive and prone to worry, idealistic and peaceable, sociable and curious, and having general aesthetic interests. IPAR described these as psychologically complex and inner directed, intellectually able and interested. They were seen to value cognitive pursuits and to derive important satisfactions from such work and achievements. They showed concern with philosophical problems, but not necessarily in only an abstract, disinterested way. They frequently took stands on moral issues and at times showed a great deal of self-awareness and self-concern that was neither neurotic, nor immature. They were seen as socially perceptive and responsive to interpersonal nuances; these attributes showed up as good judgment and common sense.

f. Scale #6 is 67, high (Pa) Paranoia

Males with high scores were rated as sensitive, emotional, and prone to worry. They were seen as kind, affectionate, generous, and grateful. Also, sentimental, and softhearted, peaceable, cooperative, and courageous and as having wide interests. IPAR raters saw them as readily becoming ego-involved, and tending to make these pursuits personally relevant and important. Also, energetic and industrious, and as showing high initiative, poised, rational, and clear thinking, intelligent, and insightful, with wide interests and progressive approaches. Self-descriptions were trustful, amorous, and worldly.

g. Scale #7 is 58, high (Pt) Psychasthenia

Peer raters found these sentimental, peaceable, and good tempered. Also verbal, individualistic, and dissatisfied. IPAR found these to be dull, formal, and unemotional. Also, idealistic, and insightful; appeared immature and quarrelsome. Self-descriptions were sentimental and high strung with general aesthetic interests and national, political interests.

h. Scale #8 is 51, high (Sc) Schizophrenia

These were rated as prone to worry, self-dissatisfied and conscientious, good tempered, versatile, and enthusiastic with wide interests and general aesthetic interests. Also, frank, fair-minded, and courageous. Appeared kind and sentimental, as well as peaceable. IPAR found them effective in communicating their ideas clearly, but showing evidence of being at odds with themselves and of having major internal conflicts. Also, hostile, blustery, irritable, resentful, touchy, moody, stubborn, opinionated, autocratic, deceitful, disorderly, and impulsive. They displayed imaginative, mischievous, and sharp-witted behavior. Self-descriptions include high strung, conscientious, worrying, individualistic, enterprising, adventurous, curious, and amorous; also, frank, talkative, kind, sentimental and grateful.

i. Scale #9 is 55, high (Ma) Hypomania

Peer ratings include adjectives sociability, energy, openness, forward, talkative, and verbal, individualistic, impulsive, enthusiastic, adventurous, and curious, with interest in national, political matters. Also, liking drinking, generous, softhearted, affectionate and sentimental. Acquaintances described as prone to worry, self-dissatisfied, and conventional. IPAR found these sensitive, thoughtful, and imaginative, as anxious and nervous, and as deceitful and unfriendly. Self-descriptions include impulsive, talkative, adventurous, liking to drink, frank, and reclusive.

j. Scale #10 is 37, low (Si) Social Introversion

These were seen as social and versatile in the sense of mixing well. Also, expressive, ebullient, colorful persons. They tended to be ostentatious and exhibitionistic, active, vigorous and competitive with their peers. They showed strong initiative and took the ascendant role in relations with others. They appeared to possess high intellectual ability and were verbally fluent and facile. They were persuasive and often won others over to their viewpoint. They also manipulated others in attempting to gain their own ends, seeing things rather opportunistically rather than sensitive to the meaning and value of these persons as individuals.

These men were seen as potentially guileful and deceitful. They emphasized oral pleasure in a self-indulgent way, seeking aesthetic and sensuous impressions. They appeared unable to delay gratification and often acted with insufficient thought and deliberation. This under control of their impulses, combined with their tendency to get ego involved in many different things, led to a characteristic aggressiveness or hostility in their personal relations.

These men emphasized success and productive achievement as a means for achieving status, recognition, and power. They readily become counterproductive in the face of frustration and easily aroused hostility and resentment in those with whom they dealt. IPAR found them active, ambitious, and blustery. Also, immature, hasty, quick, ingenious, witty, and having initiative. Self-descriptions include sociable, enterprising, enthusiastic, affectionate and responsive, courageous and cheerful, hardheaded, facing life, temperate, and adaptable.

5.8 Myers - Briggs Type Indicator-The INTJ Type

(Notice how the different test descriptions of personality reinforce each other).

The introverted intuitive is the outstanding innovator in the field of ideas. principles and systems of thought. He trusts his own intuitive insight as to the true relationships and meanings of things, regardless of established authority or popularly accepted beliefs. His faith in his inner vision of the possibilities is such that he can remove mountains - and often does. In the process, he may drive others, or oppose them, as hard as his own inspirations drive him. Problems only stimulate him; the impossible takes a little longer, but not much. His outer personality is judging, being mainly due to his auxiliary, which is T. Thus, he backs up his original insight with the determination, perseverance and enduring purpose of a judging type. He wants his ideas worked out in practice, applied and accepted, and spends any time and effort necessary to that end.

The danger for the type arise from his single-minded concentration. He sees his goal so clearly that he may miss other things that he ought to see, even though they conflict with that goal: the rights, interest, feelings and points of view of other people; facts, conditions and counter forces that do exist and must be reckoned with. He should talk over his plans with an extroverted sensing type and really listen to him.

He is outstandingly effective in scientific research and engineering design where his boldly ingenious ideas have to meet and fit reality. He always needs some such reality-check, but the very boldness of his ideas may be of immense value in any field and should not be smothered in a routine job full of details.

If his judgment is undeveloped, he cannot criticize his own inner vision, and he tends to reject judgments from outside without really hearing them. As a result, he cannot shape his inspirations into effective action, and may appear only as a visionary, or crank.

He is the "most individualistic and most independent of all the types. Resembles extroverted thinker, both in his organizing ability and in the danger of ignoring other peoples' feelings and views. Needs to make a real effort to understand and appreciate. Likely to be an effective, relentless organizer. Can be an efficient executive, rich in ideas.

"The INTJ's usually have original minds and great drive for their own ideas and purposes. In the fields that appeal to them, they have a fine power to organize a job and carry it through with, or without help. Skeptical, critical, independent, determined, sometimes stubborn. They must learn to yield less important points in order to win the most important."

6 MARRIED LIFE, FLOWERS, WORK, ARCHITECTURE, AND DEATH

As I have mentioned to you before, I met my only wife, Gloria Campbell, and we got married 2/15/67. We actually planned to marry on Valentine's Day, but that was not to be! I first saw her at my Mom's house, at 1836 South Harding Street, Chicago. She was there with my younger sister, Bobbie, and James, my younger brother.

The three of them were dancing. I checked her out: nice body, nice hips. Gloria has a beautiful face, a lovely face, and a wonderful smile. She has a good sense of humor. So, we chatted a bit.

Gloria's heritage: Her father is Puerto Rican; mother, African American, born in Chicago.

I got Gloria's phone number and address. I collected a number of phone numbers and addresses while in Chicago, to write to people of interest - mostly women. Gloria and I corresponded, after I arrived at Grand Forks AFB, in North Dakota.

When, I came home to attend Fred Robinson, Sr.'s funeral, Gloria and I saw each other again. We started seeing each other, and we decided to get married. I was 22, she was 18. We were married ten years. We have two surviving children, daughters. And the 4-year age difference, the 10 year marriage, and the two daughters is exactly what happened when I was here 200 years ago as Thomas Jefferson, third President of The United States of America! I AM THE THIRD PROGRESSION! Third child, third sign, (Gemini), Third Patriarch, (Jacob), and I am a "twin."

Gloria's (our) photo was once in the AT&T Long Lines Magazine. It was taken when I was giving a tour and presentation to visitors to AT&T. The photographer got Gloria and me in the same photo.

We used to visit the Drive-in at Cicero and Cermak, in Cicero, Illinois. We'd get the big barrels of Pop Corn, get soda, and whatever, and relax in the car, and watch the movies.

I remember when we had not been married too long. We were sitting there in the car, the Chevrolet. Gloria was feeding me popcorn, out of her hand. I told Gloria, "We haven't been married very long, and already you have me eating out of your hands? Can you guess what she told me? LOL!

Back in the day, marriage was great! Before we moved to 5312 W. Adams, we often went to a Laundry Mat to wash our clothes. I enjoyed folding clothes together! Isn't that something?

We used to go to the Jewel Store on Madison Street, I believe at Kenton Avenue, about two blocks east of Cicero Ave. I remember when that store first opened. Then, we used to get the Chablis Wines, the smoked cheese, and various other chesses. I used to enjoy flirting with Gloria, while we were shopping; sometimes we would just be waiting in line.

6.1 Our Sunday Cooking

Many, if not most Sundays, we would cook up huge meals, of many dishes. And some of this food would often last well into the week, if not all week.

There would be a huge container of Potato Salad, then maybe a Roast, or whole chicken. Then, fried okra, corn bread, greens, maybe broccoli, a cake, pies, and maybe lamb-chops, Jell-O, etc.! That was a lot of food!

6.2 My Flower Gardens, In Chicago and University Park

I used to plant and maintain a flower garden, each year, in the front and in the back yard, at 5312 W. Adams Street.

I enjoyed selecting the flowers, planting them, and maintaining them! Sometimes, they would be just gorgeous, showing off their beauty!

In University Park, I likewise maintained a flower garden, but only in the front of the house!

In Lansing, Illinois, interestingly, the neighbor to my right (north) maintains a fabulous flower garden. So the relative proximity to me and the effect is the same as if I continue to maintain a flower garden. This, and many more instances demonstrate the reality of synchronicity. That is, an individual will create an environment or align himself into an environment that reflects his inner essence. I think of it as demonstrated by electrons acquiring or giving up electrons in their outer shell – to attain stability and balance. Align or be aligned!

6.3 My Youth Motivation Program Experiences

Back in the day: In about 1973, or 1974, I started work in the Youth Motivation Program, in the High Schools of Chicago. I worked at AT&T Long Lines, and I would tell the students in a classroom what my job was like. I would tell them about AT&T. I would tell them what skills were needed in my or similar jobs. And I would encourage them to stay in school. I visited maybe nearly two-dozen different schools, and I would sometimes go back to the same school, but to a different class- room. I enjoyed this "Public Speaking," very much!

6.4 My Walking And Looking At Buildings And Structures

I used to walk around, looking at buildings, looking at the architecture. I started doing this when I was about 16 years old, and we lived at 1836 S. Harding. I used to go up to Eighteenth Street, and head west. I would look at the bungalows, the ranch style homes. I would look at the larger buildings.

When living at 5312 W. Adams, I would do this. I would head in any direction, and look! Likewise, this happened when we lived at 1044 Blackhawk Drive, in University Park.

But I also started to drive around, everywhere and look at buildings, look at structures.

At 1814 W. Division Street, I saw the building at 1816 W. Division being built from day one. And I watched some of this from the second floor: fascinating!

I maintain cell sites in Chicago, and I sometimes travel over much of Chicagoland, to restore a site or fix a problem at a site. I am responsible for McCormick Place, and from the Lakefront to past Western Avenue, from East Wacker Drive north, to about Thirty-ninth Street south. But I sometimes service other peoples' areas. I enjoy looking at and marveling at the amazing Chicago architecture!

Of course, I read Frank Lloyd Wright's book. It was about his houses, and his architectural style. I visited or drove by some of his houses in Oak Park. The other Chicago area architect I studied about is Louis Sullivan.

To see some significant architecture, from about 2600 B. C. to 20004 AD, with construction dates: **See** GreatBuildings.com online.

6.5 The Deaths of Significant People in My Life:

Big Mama passed to the other side in 1973, in Indianapolis, Indiana. There were scores of our relatives at her funeral, from east, west, north, and south! Peace and Honor and Blessings on Annie Shinault-Watson, my most beloved Big Mama!

Billie, my older sister's first born was killed here in Chicago at age 20. Billie was born in 1956. He died in 1976. I think he was bold and brash. I think he lived without fear, which is very, very good! Peace and blessings on Billie!

Jimmy Jr., in 1968. Well, you know about Jimmy Jr.! But I feel certain that Jimmy Jr. came back in the form of Runako, our second daughter.

Chuck, or Charles Jones was born June 9, 1937, and was killed in about 1990. Chuck was my dear cousin. He was a friend, someone to "shoot the breeze with!" What a loss! Peace and blessings on Charles

(Chuck) Jones!

   Mother made transition on 5/17/05, at 9:45 AM. We celebrated her life and legacy on Saturday, 5/21/05.

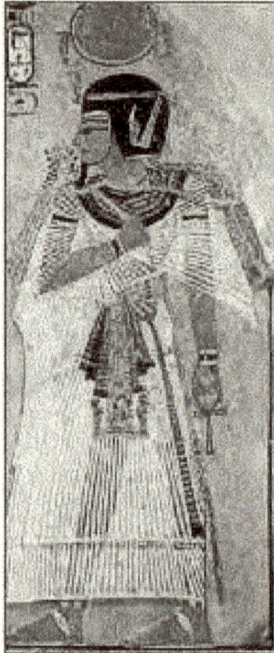

7 THOMAS JEFFERSON-THE INDISPENSABLE MAN
Thomas Jefferson Vs. Alexander Hamilton?
Re: The Debate on 2/22/05

I saw a debate on whether Thomas Jefferson or Alexander Hamilton was of greater influence on the life, character and institutions of this country, this morning, on C-SPAN or C-SPAN2.

To even seriously contemplate this question is *extremely* absurd! Jefferson is America! He is the heart and soul of America, and what the USA is destined to become! But Jefferson is primarily the good side of America! There is also an ugly or bad side! Moreover, Jeffersonian ideals are the heart, mind, and soul of what is best and good in the world!

Jefferson is sometimes very much misunderstood because of owning slaves, and not freeing any except for Sally Hemming and her family, at the time of his death, in 1826. Jefferson was born into a slave-holding society.

At the age of 14, when his father died, he inherited the 30 slaves and more than 2,500 acres of land that his father had owned. **Jefferson did not manage his estate!** His guardian John Harvey managed the estate until Jefferson came of age.

1. Born April 13, 1743 in Albemarle County, Virginia.
2. In 1760, he entered the College of William and Mary at age 16.
3. While at college, Jefferson met friends, Professor of Mathematics, William Small, Judge George Wythe, Governor Francis Fauquier, and Patrick Henry.
4. In 1762, he graduated William and Mary College, then, studied law, at about age 19.
5. In 1767, he was admitted to the bar, at about age 24.
6. Jefferson designed and supervised the building of Monticello.
Work started, 1768, and ended, 1809! It was remodeled several times between 1768 and 1809.
7. Elected to House of Burgesses in 1769, (at about age 26) and served there until 1775.

8. With friends Patrick Henry, Richard Henry Lee, and Francis Lightfoot Lee, met in Apollo Room of Williamsburg's Raleigh Tavern, in 1769, and formed non-importation association against Britain. Protested against import duties provided by Townsend Acts.

9. In 1772, he married Martha Wayles Skelton (at about age 29). She was born 1748, died 1782. *Martha brought Sally Hemming –her half-sister (and other slaves) into the Jefferson estate. Also, Sally Hemming and her children should be identified as Caucasian, not African American due to their physical appearance. Eventually, the children moved into and blended right into the Caucasian world as a choice (Note: Gloria, Khalim's wife was born in 1948.) Also note: significant aspects tend to often mirror themselves in incarnations: Jacob married two sisters, Leah and Rachel and fathered two children each through Zilpah and Bilhah, their handmaidens.* Tradition says that Jacob was a righteous man. And his wives were rivals in bearing children destined to become God's chosen, the ancient Nation of Israel.

10. In 1774, Jefferson organized another non-importation agreement. Age, 31.

11. In 1774, he called for a meeting of all the colonies to consider their grievances.

12. He was elected to represent Albemarle County at Virginia Convention, which, in turn elected Virginia delegates to the First Continental Congress.

13. Jefferson argued that the English Parliament had no right to govern America in a pamphlet called, "A Summary View of the Rights of British America," in 1774.

14. Attended second Virginia Convention, in the spring of 1775, and was chosen as a delegate to Second Continental Congress. He was about 32 years old.

15. Answered so-called message of peace from British Prime Minister, Lord North. It was called "Reply to Lord North," and rejected North's proposal for the colonies to tax themselves, instead of Parliament taxing them.

16. Daughter, Martha born in 1772. She passed away in 1836. (Note: Runako, Khalim's second daughter was born in 1972.)

17. After the war began, he was asked to draft a "Declaration of the Causes and Necessity of Taking up Arms." His version was "too strong," and John Dickinson drafted a substitute, using much of Jefferson's draft.

18. In 1776, he wrote the Declaration of Independence. He was 33 years old. Note: Youssef Khalim wrote *People of The Future/Day*, during 1976-1978, at about age 33.

19. In September, 1776, Jefferson resigned from Congress, and returned to the Virginia House of Delegates.

20. Jefferson sponsored a bill abolishing entail, in Virginia, the largest colony. Then, he sponsored a bill abolishing primogeniture, which allowed great land estates to be broken up.

21. The legislature passed another bill introduced by Jefferson, which allowed immigrants to become naturalized citizens after living in Virginia two years.

22. Jefferson also introduced bills to assure religious toleration and abolish the special privileges of the Anglican Church. Ten years later Virginia passed his **"Statute of Religious Freedom!"**

23. Jefferson proposed a system of free public education, with a state-supported university.

24. Daughter, Mary born in 1778. She passed away in 1804.

25. In 1779 and 1780, he was elected Governor of Virginia.

26. In 1783, he was elected to Congress, and chaired several committees.

27. Jefferson devised a decimal system of currency that was approved by Congress.

28. He piloted through Congress the Treaty of Paris, which ended the Revolutionary War.

29. Jefferson worked on the Ordinance of 1784, and the Land Ordinance of 1785, which form the basis of *all* later USA land policies.

30. Under Jefferson's leadership **Virginia gave up its claim to the Northwest Territory, in 1784. Other States followed suit, and the Northwest Territory was created!**

31. Jefferson chaired both Congressional Committees that looked at how to govern the Northwest Territory, and how to dispose of

its land. The result was an Ordinance of 1784. It formed the basis of the "Northwest Ordinance of 1787."

32. In 1785, he was appointed Minister to France. Martha went with him.

33. While in France, Jefferson proposed a **Charter of Rights**, to be presented to the king.

34. Mary joined them in 1787, and she brought Sally Hemming along.

35. He apparently began the intimate relationship with Sally Hemming, in France – where she was a free person. (There was no slavery in France.) Sally was born in 1773 and passed away in 1835.

36. In 1787, Statesmen assembled in convention and drew up a new constitution. James Madison sent Jefferson a draft copy. **Jefferson objected strongly to it not having a bill of rights, and urged one.** Consequently, James Madison introduced the 10 Amendments that became known as the Bill of Rights.

37. Jefferson applied for a leave, and sailed for home in October, 1789.

38. In 1789, he became Secretary of State, as requested by George Washington.

39. When Jefferson was Secretary of State, he developed his "strict construction" theory of the constitution when differences arose vis-à-vis Alexander Hamilton and a National Bank, Revolutionary War debts, etc.

40. Jefferson led the Democratic-Republicans, called Republicans at the time, though later they became the Democratic Party.

41. Jefferson tried to persuade the British to abandon their forts in the Northwest Territory.

42. In 1790, Thomas Hemming, the first of seven children, was born to Sally Hemming and Thomas Jefferson. Thomas died in 1879. The seven included Edy, in 1796, Harriet, in 1795, Beverly, in 1798, Harriet, in 1801, Madison, in 1805, and Eston, in 1808.

43. In January, 1794, Jefferson returned to Monticello.

44. By late 1796, Jefferson had become alarmed over the centralizing

tendencies of the government. **He accepted the Democratic-Republican nomination for president and ran against the Federalist candidate, John Adams.**

45. In 1796, he was elected Vice-president of the USA, with 68 electoral votes to Adam's 71 votes.

46. Relations with Adams grew more strained, and broke in 1800.

47. To aid Congressional deliberations when he presided over the Senate, Jefferson wrote the **Manual of Parliamentary Practice**, which is still in use.

48. Jefferson opposed the Alien and Sedition Acts of 1798 (which deprived the Democratic-Republicans of **freedom of speech, and of the press** with the "compact" theory of the Union.)

49. In 1801, he was **elected President of the USA, getting 73 electoral votes to 65 for John Adams. Congress decided, on the 36th Ballot!**

50. Jefferson was the first president to be inaugurated in Washington! 12 of the 73 votes came from those held in bondage in the Slave-holding States, and this further made African Americans inheritors of, and heirs to the promise of America.

51. Jefferson's grandson, James Randolph, was the first child born in the White House.

52. Jefferson kept a French chef and steward in the White House.

53. He introduced shaking hands instead of bowing before the president. He placed dinner guests at a round table, so everyone would feel equally important!

54. He said the **election of 1800 was as much of a real revolution in the *principles* of government as was the declaration of 1776 was in form.**

55. The USA flag had 15 stars throughout Jefferson's term of office.

56. In 1802, Congress established the US Military Academy at West Point, NY.

57. In 1803, the U. S. purchased the Louisiana Territory for about $15,000,000, and doubled the size of the USA!

58. In *1803, Jefferson got a grant from Congress for the Lewis and Clark Expedition.* **The exploration strengthened the claim of the United States on the Oregon Territory, and finally, led to the US expansion to the Pacific Ocean!**

59. Jefferson developed some ideas for the addition of east and west terraces, and a north portico to the White House. He employed Benjamin Latrobe to execute them.

60. In **1804, Jefferson was reelected with 162 electoral votes to 14, for his Federalist opponent.** *12 of the 162 votes came from those held in bondage in the Slave-holding States, and this further made African Americans inheritors of, and heirs to the promise of America.*

61. In 1811, Jefferson reconciled with John Adams.

62. In 1815, Jefferson sold 6,400 books to Congress to replace those destroyed when the British attacked the capitol,

63. In 1819, he founded the University of Virginia. It opened in 1825, with 40 students.

64. On July 4, 1826, on the 50th Anniversary (Jubilee Year) of the Declaration of Independence, he transitioned from this world along with his good friend, John Adams – which is obviously a miracle!

65. On 8/4-5/1999, I confirmed my incarnation (during meditation), as Thomas Jefferson, third president of the United States! See *The Resurrection of Noah!*

66. On 2/23/02, I learned and confirmed that Thomas Jefferson is the reincarnation of Jacob, also known as Israel, and father of the 12 boys that became known as the Nation of Israel. **See** *The Resurrection of Noah!*

67. On 5/2/2000, I learned that Prophet Muhammad is the reincarnation of Moses, and he is highly esteemed and honored in the spiritual world, or heaven! See *The Resurrection of Noah!*

68. There is none other like Thomas Jefferson! And, there is no God, but God! And you will be hard pressed to find anybody who remotely compares to Thomas Jefferson!

8 MODELS, FRIENDS, AND LOVERS

8.1 Marsha

I met Marsha Ward in the spring of 1976, through her cousin, Denise. The first thing I tried to give her was the album by Stevie Wonder, *Songs In The Key Of Life*. She already had a copy!

Marsha worked in the drug store, on one of the lower levels of The Sears Tower building, in downtown Chicago, on Franklin Avenue.

We sat and had drinks in a lounge, maybe a few doors away, and around a corner from the store where she worked. Actually, I first pursued her cousin, Denise. We went out on a date or two.

I come on kind of strong sometimes! I think Marsha ended up mediating, or explaining me to Denise. I ended up seeing Marsha, and being more and more interested in Marsha.

Marsha and I hit it off from the start. I remember once we went into a woman's clothing store in Sears Tower. She was posing, accentuating her hips, showing off her figure – having fun! Marsha was always a lot of fun to be with!

I never saw her angry. She was very beautiful, and seemed very attractive to me, even when she said she was upset!

I remember her coming up to visit me in the employee lounge at 10 South Canal Street, Chicago. She looked shy, vulnerable, sweet. She wore some kind of cap (or hat).

I remember seeing her in a flowing, maybe beige dress, with mild orange designs (or flowers on it), sitting next to me in our vehicle, in the park by Sixty-Eighth Street, just sitting there talking, seeing boats in the distance.

It was springtime. The trees and flowers were showing off! Her eyes:
were green and hazel, beautiful, and lovely - just like spring!

She said she was upset because I was teasing her, or somehow
provoking her. She didn't look upset at all, just attractive and desirable,
kissable, lovable!

I fell very much in-love with Marsha! And no kidding, magical things
used to happen when we were together. Honest to goodness! We had an 8-
Track Tape, by the Commodores. It disappeared, and reappeared some
days later. We probably practiced Tantra without realizing exactly what we
were doing!

Were you ever with someone for the first time, and you wanted to
leave their fragrance, the scent, and smell of them, on you –at least for an
extended, yet reasonable time? That's how it was when I was first with
Marsha!

Anyhow, sometimes relatives interfere in younger people's lives. And so
it was here! I only found out about that interference about 12 years after it
happened.

Anyway, we have to move on. There are people to meet, places to see!

8.2 Audrey

I met Audrey Bennett at 10 South Canal Street, Chicago. She worked
for Illinois Bell. I remember first seeing her on the elevator. She looked
ethnic, maybe Hispanic. She was a Sister.

We first went out to Hugh Hefner's Mansion, in or near the Rush Street
area, to see a movie that somehow was to benefit charity. I got those tickets
from Elma Robinson, my former manager.

Audrey looked very sexy and gorgeous in her dress. I think it was
black! I thought she was the most beautiful, sexy, and gorgeous woman at
the reception!

We dated for a while, went out to dance, eat. We spent a lot of time
indoors – it was fun! So much so that I again contacted Audrey in 1984.
And you have the narrative about 1984 and University Park, don't you?

8.3 Jean

I met Jean Cox at the Public Access Cable Studio, in University Park.
Jean helped me learn some things about editing film and operating the
various equipment in the studio: the lights, tapes, audio controls, and the
cameras.

Jean was very helpful quite often, and wild and free – to make life exciting! It's good to be wild sometimes, because those are the times that you will treasure in the future – and never forget! Couples should get wild with each other occasionally. Do the unexpected! Just get wild!

Did you ever have someone in your life that you would like to keep around, as a mistress? Every man should have a Jean Cox in his life - at least for a while.

8.4 Menai

Menai Edwards. A friend, a neighbor. I used to see her pass by. She looked fabulous! She came inside, but did not linger. There seems to be a level and type of energy that the Yogi, the Shaman has. Maybe it is not compatible with everyone.

8.5 Kathy

Kathy Bishton is the mother of my adorable son, Noah! We are very, very happy to have Noah here! And we are very grateful, thankful, and hopeful!

8.6 Kathy

Kathy Rodriquez and I go way back, to lives way in the past. Thanks for everything!

8.7 Cathy

Cathy Costner was a very good model, a friend, and a little more than that! I knew her in a previous lifetime, in Japan (for sure!)

8.8 Melovee

Melovee Schoffner was a teacher at Thomas Jefferson Elementary, 1522 West Fillmore, Chicago. Yes, that School! But, I met her at Loop City College, in 1973.

Melovee reminds me of how Rosa looked. Do some of us look like those peoples from the Indian subcontinent, or do they look like us? And do those peoples call themselves a *color*? People over here need to wise up!

I started dealing with Melovee when my marriage did not seem very promising. One morning, coming from her house, in Evanston, I was traveling in our lovely, blue, white-leather interior, Cutlass Supreme. I cut onto I290, heading west and approached Ashland Ave.

A 1-foot rectangular stone boulder crashed into the front passenger side window of the car! Dust, glass, what seemed like smoke filled the right side of the car! Boy, did I let Melovee go! But fast! I took that as a hint from God! LOL!

Melovee did phone after that! Once, I think Gloria caught us talking on the phone. She got a *little* upset! She tore many of my Tarot cards in half! LOL! I still have them, but somewhat repaired! Gloria didn't think it was so funny at the time!

8.9 Lorraine

I had a vision about Lorraine, a day or so before I met her. It was a very wonderful vision. And it came true, almost exactly! Some of it was symbolic though.

I met Lorraine Scott at Marty and Don Sladek's house, in Downers Grove, Illinois.

Sometimes you meet someone who is therapy, healing, and growth for you. I think Marsha and Lorraine fit that bill. Again, I want to mention that my level and quality of energy seems to be unique, maybe because of the yoga, shamanism, and the spirituality that I have.

I have been told that the woman feels strange, a day or more following our encounter. At least one individual experienced something more traumatic – almost like a seizure!

After Lorraine, came the torrential rains, a flood, on 7/20/1980. **Note: I am an Initiate!** I saw the larvae shortly afterwards. The worm morphs (dies), and turns into a fly! I know what that means. Can *you* figure it out?

A hint on how to die, and be born again: We have to genuinely love, respect, and treat others *exactly* like we want to be treated – no exceptions!

My experiences with Lorraine were short-lived. Our mutual friends said she soon joined the Air Force – Aim High!

8.10 Anita

I met Anita Branch at a social service agency, located at about Cicero Avenue and Madison Street, Chicago. She helped me incorporate our organization (Afrikan Kongress International, AKI) in July, 1979.

Nice experience, good experience. Anita was/is a wonderful person. And I am very grateful for having known her.

8.11 Beverly

I met Beverly Shannon at the Jewel Food store on Madison Street, near Central. Beverly used to visit us often, in University Park.

We were friends, probably should have been much better friends. She had the bluest, baby-blue eyes, for a sister!

8.12 Tamara

I met Tamara at a fast food place on Madison Street, near Lockwood, in Chicago. She became a family friend. She used to come over to our house on West Adams St. And she came out to University Park once.

We used to use tons of models: Brenda Trotter, Pat Phillips, Martha, and others.

8.13 Melody

Melody Knight was/is a special friend, and my brother, James, has remained in touch with her.

I met Melody Knight at Sears Roebuck, in Chicago, on Homan Avenue. She used to work in the Catalog Sales Department.

Melody is/was a very wonderful person, a nice person, a good person; very dependable and responsible. I understand she is now the Principal of a school in Chicago!

What gorgeous eyes; very intriguing, very lovely. Great posture, great "walk!" Beautiful lady! We were eager to have Melody model for our first book.

9 GLORIA'S SISTERS; TALK, THEN SILENCE

I want to mention a word or two here about the Campbell Sisters, the sisters of Gloria, the only woman I was ever married to.

Gloria was the oldest. She is four years younger than me, just like Martha Wayles Skelton, my wife as Jefferson.

Next, there is Diane; then, Kitty, and finally Gaye. The only brother I became somewhat familiar with is named Stan. But there was a still younger brother, named Larry. You understand, they were all younger than me. And very few people are like me. I am a working class Intellectual! From the time I came to Chicago and became aware of and interested in the arts, politics, music, architecture, and the world, I came into my own. PEOPLE ARE BORN as WHO THEY ARE! But, they kind of **grow *into* who they are!** So, I became a Renaissance Man, **because I was *that* previously!**

When we lived on Adams, in the early years, Kitty lived with us for a short while. And Gaye lived with us for a short while.

Kitty became a teacher. She retired as a counselor in The Public School System of Chicago. I talked to Kitty more than the other sisters. We used to debate and discuss some of the things I was interested in, politics, religion, writing, etc.

(Female friends are special. When a bunch of males get together, socially, they are often crude and obscene. Therefore I have often preferred the company of learned men, or men engaged in business and commerce, or the company of female friends. *They look better, are not crude, and they smell good!*)

Diane was once a Centerfold in Jet Magazine. She used to keep a lounge on Chicago's Southside.

Larry borrowed our Plymouth Barracuda. Unknown to Gloria and I at the time, he had an accident in it. The "Reverse" Transmission gear was disabled when he returned the car.

Anyway, many of the Campbell children used to get together. Gloria and Diane formed the nucleus of a Social Club. They played cards, had meetings, or partied.

And what about me? I did everything with Tonya and Runako. They went almost everywhere I went! There were Ballet lessons, and Tumbling classes. We visited museums, and the Adler Planetarium. We did homework together, or engaged in Extra Curricula school activities. I frequently took them to work with me on weekends. And we visited Lou's Bookshelf, Haki's place, where intellectuals met. Or we visited the Inner City Studies Building, on East Oakwood Boulevard.

My brother James, and/or Chuck, our cousin, and I used to talk politics and/or religion. Chuck was once an ordained minister.

Since I was *not* interested in a lot of the activities of many of my relatives, they sometimes called me anti-social, or stand-offish. I can be hermitic, ascetic. I can practice silence. Sometimes I am a Motor Mouth. When I learned that Jefferson would not communicate with Adams, for years – this too (and many more examples like it) show that I have not changed too much in many ways, in 200 years!

10 CORRUPT FORMER GOVERNOR, JIM EDGAR, AND THE CRIMINALS AT DCFS

Here an observation: When you get older, wiser, you think differently. You moderate your views. At some point you may think about how nice it would be to hang the human beasts, the lying, degenerate thugs who stole Noah. And then they did a cover-up, worse than Water Gate. The U.S. Attorney in Illinois at the time, Jim Burns, knew it. ACLU knew it! (They were party to the Consent Decree involving The Federal Court, in 1983.) Rainbow Push knew it! Carol Mosely Braun knew it! Emile Jones knew it! Former Governor, Jim Thompson, and his law firm knew it! Many public officials in Illinois, and in the USA knew it!

Many people sell out! And they sell out with their silence! They sell their soul to the devil! And there will be wailing and gnashing of teeth!

These criminals include former Governor of Illinois, Jim Edgar, and Charlene Necco, and Genie Marco, of DCFS.

The world should know this: The Judicial System of Illinois, and the USA are extremely corrupt! The USA is an *extreme* tyranny, like the Bible says. Read the description of the Seventh and Eighth World Powers in the Books of Daniel and Revelation, sometimes called Babylon, the Great. Also, understand that the USA is a renewal or Renaissance of Greece and Rome. Most of the "good" part was grafted onto that monster by Thomas Jefferson and other good people. The USA is also the real Israel – bringing that good and bad aspect into its nature and character.

11 REINCARNATION IS LIKE AN OAK TREE IN CHICAGO

The oak tree's leaves show their age in the fall. They lose their illustrious greenness, and turn various colors in their last, dying days. They *go to sleep* during the winter. But, when spring comes, *they retrace their pattern* of previous years. They sprout buds, flowers, stems, and limbs almost *exactly* where they existed before. And they become quite alive!

Then, they may grow new limbs, new branches. They branch out into new territory! And their girth, trunks, and *roots* get bigger!

What have you done for me lately? Nature, or God, wants to know, So, in order to maintain a conscious, alive, earthly form, we have to continue to *produce* for Nature, produce for God! Then, having been producers in God's *Will-to-do-Good*, forever, we shall live forever!

11.1 I Had to Have It: Serpent Power

When I was about 7 years old, Fred (I believe) and I were returning to our house on the Bishop Plantation. We were walking down the dirt road, less than half a block from our house. I started spinning myself around, to make myself *high* (dizzy)! I kept doing this, over and over! I spun around faster, faster!

I stumbled, tumbled, teetered, and lunged into the barbed wire fence-that fenced in the pasture, on the left side of the road!

The steel barbs tore into my left arm, my face, and my left thigh! I was a bloody mess! They patched me up, and all was well. But, the scars are still there, but not too noticeable, and they never disadvantaged me in any recognizable way. I generally never think about that incident.

In 1971, in the summer, I started practicing yoga. We lived at 5312 W. Adams St. I started with classes, down on Michigan Avenue, at the Sivananda Yoga Center! Yoga (Unity) is a kind of **controlled**, *natural high*, or quickening, induced through mental discipline, and physical and breathing exercises. Consciousness changes, improves!

Right away I noticed that when we did relaxation exercises, my consciousness drifted into a heavenly, blissful state. And back on Adams Street, on our back porch, I tried to do the Sun Exercise. When I would lean way back, I used to fall out - blissfully, on the back porch: Baloom, loom, loom! Over and over, I would do this, time after time - until it did not knock me out anymore! Gloria was at first concerned. But what could she do? I had to have it - Serpent Power!

In yoga, we raise the Kundalini, or Serpent Power, lying curled up, at the base of the spine. We raise it up and up, through the seven Chakras, and when (if) we fully succeed, it gives us this Universal Consciousness, or awareness, sort of like the serpent in the Garden of Eden had. But we use our consciousness and awareness for good, because there is cause/ effect, action/reaction, and what you sow, you will surely reap!

First, though, just a little background: before I started practicing yoga, I got all my affairs in order, my financial, and my social, and my family affairs. I was determined to get yoga – Unity, Serpent Power! No, I would not to be denied!

And as I have related to you elsewhere, I attained (I believe) full and complete Unity on July 20, 1980!

In the years before full Unity, and in the years afterward, I have the power to "Time", or Astral Travel! Some nights, I can just lie still, close my eyes, and look into the "Heavens," and look at "the stars!" And I hope to maintain Unity and good standing with God, our Creator, forever and ever more!

I suspect that everything that God created will turn out for the better – eventually, or we will erase it (them) from the universe!

The New Testament, The Gospels, say that Jesus is the likeness (reincarnation) of Adam. So does the Qur'an!

Jesus overcame his shortcomings as Adam. He challenged those current rulers of the planet, the Serpents, descendants of reptiles. He recognized them for what they are!

Today, they are still the rulers over mankind. They are the liars, warmongers, the militarists, the George Bushes, and his Reptile Family, Donald Rumsfeld, and the racist oppressors in the State of Israel: *you will know them by their fruit!*

But today, we (God) will take back our planet! And, we will bind the reptiles (and George Bushes) for 1000 years! I, too have Serpent Power! And when we fight the reptiles, when we give tit-for-tat, WE ALWAYS WIN!

11.2 Jesus Went-Off On The Reptiles

Matt. 23

[1] Then spake Jesus to the multitude, and to his disciples,

[2] Saying, The scribes and the Pharisees sit in Moses' seat:

[3] All therefore whatsoever they bid you observe, that observe and do; but do not ye after their works: for they say, and do not.

74

[4] For they bind heavy burdens and grievous to be borne, and lay them on men's shoulders; but they themselves will not move them with one of their fingers.

[5] But all their works they do for to be seen of men: they make broad their phylacteries, and enlarge the borders of their garments,

[6] And love the uppermost rooms at feasts, and the chief seats in the synagogues,

[7] And greetings in the markets, and to be called of men, Rabbi, Rabbi.

[8] But be not ye called Rabbi: for one is your Master, even Christ; and all ye are brethren.

[9] And call no man your father upon the earth: for one is your Father, which is in heaven.

[10] Neither be ye called masters: for one is your Master, even Christ.

[11] But he that is greatest among you shall be your servant.

[12] And whosoever shall exalt himself shall be abased; and **he that shall humble himself shall be exalted.**

[13] **But woe unto you, scribes and Pharisees, hypocrites**! for ye shut up the kingdom of heaven against men: for ye neither go in your- selves, neither suffer ye them that are entering to go in.

[14] **Woe unto you, scribes and Pharisees, hypocrites!** for ye devour widows' houses, and for a pretense make long prayer: therefore ye shall receive the greater damnation.

[15] **Woe unto you, scribes and Pharisees, hypocrites!** for ye compass sea and land to make one proselyte, and when he is made, ye make him twofold more the child of hell than yourselves.

[16] **Woe unto you, ye blind guides,** which say, Whosoever shall swear by the temple, it is nothing; but whosoever shall swear by the gold of the temple, he is a debtor!

[17] **Ye fools and blind**: for whether is greater, the gold, or the temple that sanctifieth the gold?

[18] And, Whosoever shall swear by the altar, it is nothing; but whoso- ever sweareth by the gift that is upon it, he is guilty.

[19] **Ye fools and blind**: for whether is greater, the gift, or the altar that sanctifieth the gift?

[20] Whoso therefore shall swear by the altar, sweareth by it, and by all things thereon.

[21] And whoso shall swear by the temple, sweareth by it, and by him that dwelleth therein.

[22] And he that shall swear by heaven sweareth by the throne of God, and by him that sitteth thereon.

[23] **Woe unto you, scribes and Pharisees, hypocrites!** for ye pay tithe of mint and anise and cummin, and have omitted the weightier matters of the law, judgment, mercy, and faith: these ought ye to have done, and not to leave the other undone.

[24] **Ye blind guides, which strain at a gnat, and swallow a camel.**

[25] **Woe unto you, scribes and Pharisees, hypocrites!** for ye make clean the outside of the cup and of the platter, but within they are full of extortion and excess.

[26] **Thou blind Pharisee,** cleanse first that which is within the cup and platter, that the outside of them may be clean also.

[27] **Woe unto you, scribes and Pharisees, hypocrites**! for ye are like unto whited sepulchers, which indeed appear beautiful outward, **but are within full of dead men's bones, and of all uncleanness.**

[28] Even so ye also outwardly appear righteous unto men, but **within ye are full of hypocrisy and iniquity.**

[29] **Woe unto you, scribes and Pharisees, hypocrites!** because ye build the tombs of the prophets, and garnish the sepulchers of the righteous,

[30] And say, If we had been in the days of our fathers, we would not have been partakers with them in the blood of the prophets.

[31] Wherefore ye be witnesses unto yourselves, that ye are the children of them which killed the prophets.

[32] Fill ye up then the measure of your fathers.

[33] Ye serpents, ye generation of vipers, how can ye escape the damnation of hell?

[34] Wherefore, behold, I send unto you prophets, and wise men, and scribes: and some of them ye shall kill and crucify; and some of them shall ye scourge in your synagogues, and persecute them from city to city:

[35] That upon you may come all the righteous blood shed upon the earth, from the blood of righteous Abel unto the blood of Zacharias son of Barachias, whom ye slew between the temple and the altar.

[36] Verily I say unto you, All these things shall come upon this generation.

[37] O Jerusalem, Jerusalem, thou that killest the prophets, and stonest them which are sent unto thee, how often would I have gathered thy children together, even as a hen gathereth her chickens under her wings, and ye would not!

[38] Behold, your house is left unto you desolate.

[39] For I say unto you, Ye shall not see me henceforth, till ye shall say, Blessed is he that cometh in the name of the Lord.

11.3 An Exercise: We Love Everybody, And Forgive Everything

Periodically, in yoga we do cleansing exercises. We give love to the whole universe, we forgive everybody for everything – and afterwards, we decide where, or if we will get even! LOL!

This sounds like a contradiction, but what I mean is that we still – afterwards recognize that we have to exact justice, settle scores, and right wrongs on this planet! We are practical people. We may even love you, but have to kill you, destroy you, because you are like a cancer, a sore, an abomination!

Usually, we are very kind, gentle, humble, fair, just, generous, forgiving, and all that kind of stuff. When that does not work with you, it's time to kill you! Erase all trace of you from the universe – forever!

Seriously, this is how this works: We forgive everybody for everything, EVERYTHING! We repent, try *not* to make the same mistake(s) again, and we try to do better. And we keep trying! We keep striving! We seek to forgive and be forgiven.

When others seek remission, and show a change in conduct after transgressions against us– then we let it go! We try to forgive MORE than we are forgiven!

Recently, I did such a Cleansing Exercise: Forgiving everybody for everything! But, I have to settle some scores!

I love you, Glorious Gloria! I will always love you, my only wife, and mother of our beautiful daughters, Tonya and Runako!

Aha! There are other people that I have to give some love to, settle some scores:

OK, I love you! I will always love you:

Marsha Ward, my lovely, gorgeous friend, a soul mate
Audrey Bennett, my lovely, gorgeous friend
Loraine Scott, my lovely, gorgeous friend, perhaps a soul mate, with Serpent Power
Anita Branch, my lovely, gorgeous friend
Larisa, my lovely, gorgeous friend
Svetlana Korzinkina, my lovely, gorgeous friend
Ekaterina Ivanova, my lovely, gorgeous friend
Jackie Moody, my lovely friend and coworker
Kathy Bishton, the mother of my heart (Noah)
Margaret, my lovely, gorgeous friend
Shaheen, my lovely, sexy, gorgeous friend, and coworker

Lori, my lovely, sexy, gorgeous friend
Dorothy Mae Hunter, my most beloved sister
Bobbie Jean Watson, my most beloved sister
Svetlana Pirvu, my lovely, gorgeous friend
Alina Pirvu, my lovely, gorgeous friend
Galina Zaharova, my lovely, sexy, gorgeous friend
Melody Knight, my lovely, sexy, gorgeous friend
Natalia Kudryavceva, my lovely, sexy, gorgeous friend
Ruby Lee Robinson, (Mi Mom, my heart)
Tonya Robinson, my most beloved daughter
Runako Robinson, my most beloved daughter
Elma Robinson: my lovely, beautiful, & gorgeous friend and manager at AT&T Long Lines
Dorothy Malone, my beautiful and lovely friend at Wright City College
Brenda Washington, my lovely friend at Wright City College
Alma Jenkins, my lovely, beautiful, and gorgeous friend at AT&T Long Lines
Brenda Trotter, my lovely, beautiful, and gorgeous friend at AT&T Long Lines
Martha, my lovely, beautiful, and gorgeous friend at AT&T Long Lines
Jean Cox, my lovely friend from University Park Public Access Cable
Gwendolyn Brooks, my angel, my idol, a role model for mankind
Marti Sladek, my lovely friend and facilitator, from AT&T Long Lines
Teresa Mazur, my lovely, gorgeous friend
Doreen Hunter, my lovely niece
Linda Hunter, my lovely niece
Cathy Costner, my lovely friend: we go back to times in Japan together
Beverly Shannon, my lovely, sexy, gorgeous friend
Rosa: Rosa, Rosa, my ideal
Ann Barber, my lovely, gorgeous friend
Tamara, my lovely friend
Alla Gurtovenco, my lovely, gorgeous friend
Juanita Gillespie, my most beloved sister
Gloria Gillespie, my lovely niece
Kathy Rodriguez, my lovely, sexy friend: we go way back in time together
Catherine Williams, Chuck's beautiful and lovely wife
Frankie Williams, Chuck's beautiful and lovely sister-in-law
Melovee Schoffner, I'm afraid to show too much love to you, Melovee! LOL! OK, I will always love you too, Melovee! LOL!

78

12 WAS THOMAS JEFFERSON AN EQUAL OPPORTUNITY ENSLAVER?

I have already mentioned that Thomas Jefferson was born into a slave-holding society. He inherited his father's estate when his father died. He was 14 years old.

Jefferson did not manage his estate! His guardian John Harvey managed the estate until Jefferson came of age. When he was 29 years old, Jefferson's wife, Martha, brought additional persons in-bondage, into their estate, including Sally Hemming.

Genealogically, Sally Hemming, and many others on the Jefferson estate were half-or-more Caucasian. Three of Sally Hemming's four children just passed right into the Caucasian world, indistinguishable from them – two of them prior to Jefferson's passing. The last, Eston, passed into Caucasian society, when Sally Hemming died, in 1835. All three were listed on the 1830 census as Caucasian. There are references to many of the "slaves" on Jefferson's estate being Caucasian. It is obvious that you cannot just slip into Caucasian society unless for all practical purposes, you are Caucasian.

Sally Hemming was not, and is not African American. She was half or more Caucasian. That makes her Caucasian!

So, our beloved and honored Jefferson was an Equal Opportunity Enslaver, enslaving Caucasians and Africans alike!

Actually, TJ inherited most of those in nominal bondage on his estate. In the case of Sally's children, the boys were all trained as carpenters. They were trained on the violin. They were trained to be responsible, productive, and honorable members of society, starting before age ten. The daughter, Harriet, was likewise trained, but in a manner suitable for women.

Was there a kind of (wink, wink) nominal bondage on the Jefferson estate, but in reality, something very different? Was the nominal bond-age, in part, more a pretense, reflecting the outside pressures of a society gone mad over race - just like the USA is INSANE about "race" today?

TJ tried to get rid of slavery. And he tried other ameliorating (corrective) actions, to help resolve slavery and its hideous effects. The wise among us know there are things they can change! They know there are things they *cannot* change. They know how to tell the difference! And yes, we can, we should always have done more!

I recently read most of Annette Gordon-Reed's book about Sally and Thomas. In it, Jefferson's nephew, Randolph, tells of an occasion when he and his Grandfather were walking down a road together. They approached an African American man, and the man raised his hat and bowed. Thomas Jefferson responded to the man by doing the same thing. Randolph did not respond, but kept walking. Whereupon, Thomas Jefferson asked "if I (Randolph) permitted an African American to be more of a gentleman than myself."

I am still the same, 200 years later - fair, just, reciprocal, kind, humanitarian, egalitarian, and generous!

Thomas Jefferson is also Jacob! So, he is the father of all mankind. At least that is what the scriptures say. He was at least subconsciously aware of being a "Son of God!" See? Son of Geoffrey, just as I am, in this lifetime, a Son of Samuel (or God). See? Samuel means, "His name is God; name of God; God hath heard."

We are *supposed to* not have relations with just anybody, but optimally fellow Children of God!

We learned in the story of the Garden of Eden that "others" can be our mortal enemies! "Other species are not compatible with our kind. There are people who are compatible to us! There are people (or things) or diseases that we can catch from others that can kill us!"

Just consider today how we have tried to determine compatibilities by testing and comparing two or more individuals.

We used to ask, "What's your sign?"

We know today that if we catch certain diseases through sexual relations – they will simply kill us! Today, we know more about Small Pox, Malaria, tuberculosis, and other diseases. We know that some of these diseases are communicable. We would certainly have a concern, if not fear, that *the other* might have something, or they might be something – that may harm, or even kill us!

We also know that some blood types are compatible with other blood types. If a certain blood type is given to the wrong recipient, it could injure or kill him!

Jefferson knew some of this, but some of it was known on a more subconscious level. We all know things on a subconscious level.

In Jefferson's world, when he was Jacob, they were particular about who they married, or had intimate relations with. Rachel and Leah were relatives. They were cousins of Jacob.

This is why some are racist, and/or bigots today. They have a fear of the other, of the unknown, because subconsciously, they know the other can kill or injure them. Of course **much of this is unwarranted**. And today, we know you cannot judge a book by its cover!

On an evolutionary basis, some of our ancestors are possibly reptiles, some are mammals. Almost all of us are hybrids. The scriptures say mostly "reptiles" – those in rebellion against God, rule us over. They lie, cheat, steal,

80

kill, make war, and deny responsibility for their actions. George Bush belongs to such a family of reptiles, and they do the bidding of the snakes! You can tell them by their fruit!

Who are we? **We are the Children of God!** You don't believe me? It is even in the symbols, of the names: Jefferson, Thomas, Jacob, Israel, James, Lee, Robinson, Samuel (my father) – and it is true in the practical applications, in the acts, deeds, aspirations, and in the experiences. Go look it up!

And *look* at Vanessa Williams, Marsha Ward, Melody Knight, Alma Jenkins, Elma Robinson, Beverly Shannon, Haki Madhubuti, and others -and *stop* calling yourself a color: Be the Children of God!

For we know that individuals incarnate into many, if not all the races. We believe that the same soul can incarnate as male or female. We no longer have an excuse to be racist or bigoted, because you cannot judge a book by its cover!

The preoccupation with so-called race in this age, by superficial people is spoken of in the Book of Daniel, Chapter 2:

[**41**] And whereas thou sawest the feet and toes, part of potters' clay, and part of iron, **the kingdom shall be divided; but there shall be in it of the strength of the iron, forasmuch as thou sawest the iron mixed with miry clay.**

[**42**] And as the toes of the feet were part of iron, and part of clay, so the kingdom shall be partly strong, and partly broken.

[**43**] And whereas thou sawest iron mixed with miry clay**, they shall mingle themselves with the seed of men: but they shall not cleave one to another, even as iron is not mixed with clay.**

[**44**] **And** in the days of these kings shall the God of heaven set up a kingdom, which shall never be destroyed: and the kingdom shall not be left to other people, but it shall break in pieces and consume all these kingdoms, and it shall stand for ever.

[**45**] Forasmuch as thou sawest that the stone was cut out of the mountain without hands, and that it brake in pieces the iron, the brass, the clay, the silver, and the gold; the great God hath made known to the king what shall come to pass hereafter: and the dream is certain, and the interpretation thereof sure.

[**46**] Then the king Nebuchadnezzar fell upon his face, and worshipped Daniel, and commanded that they should offer an oblation and sweet odours unto him.

13 SO WHAT DOES THE BIBLE SAY ABOUT EVOLUTION, REINCARNATION?

In The Book of Genesis, the cool, green snake dropped in on Eve.

"Yo, Eve! What's happening? How you doing today?

"I'm fine! How you doing, snake?"

"I'm sliding and grooving, checking out what's happening! You sure look lovely today! Anyway, where's Adam?"

"I don't know where he is now. Why don't you look around? He shouldn't be very far from here."

"I'll look for 'em later. You, know, there's something I've been wanting to tell you. You are one fine woman! You are gorgeous, intelligent, smart, beautiful, lovely…."

"OK, I get the point! But what *is* your point?" "You know, Eve, we could all improve, grow, *excel*!

"Let me get down to the real nitty-gritty. Let me get down to the point: It's about this beautiful, amazing tree – I mean the fruit of it. It's delicious! Wow! And the effect it will have on your consciousness is amazing! It will be AWESOME! Check it out! Eve, this will improve you, open your eyes! You know what they say, 'An apple a day keeps the devil (I mean doctor) away!' He, he ha, ha!"

"Adam and I were told not to eat the fruit of that tree. We were told we would die if we ate those apples."

"Naa! You won't die! *They* know that when you eat the fruit, you will know good from evil. Your eyes will be open, and you will be wise just like *they* are!"

And so the story goes! Eve is seduced, eats the apple and introduces it to Adam, so he can break the rules too! Thereafter, Eve has to be subordinate to Adam, have pain and trauma in childbirth. And snakes and people will be afraid of each other, and enemies to each other forevermore.

The destinies of "the snake" and man supposedly crossed in the past. Will their destinies cross into the future – forever? Actually, the story in Genesis is allegory, but reflects certain realities. Through evolution, the reptile and the mammal may have gotten into each other's business and into each other's affairs. Some may conjecture that we are primarily hybrids (a mixture) of reptile and mammal.

Some of us are made in the image and likeness of God. And some of us are snakes! The Bible is allegory, parable, factual, specific, and generalization – in its various parts, sections, chapters, and verses. All of it is not to be taken literally!

The story of Adam and Eve is instructive on many levels, as is the story of creation itself. First, there are gods, and there is God! In, Genesis, in the King James Version, these distinctions between god and God are most often *not* made. See? The "Bible" was made, in part for the masses, not the Initiates!

What if the story is actually about seduction, adultery, Tantra, Yoga, and how one opens the Third Eye? Perhaps there is actually a graphic description, and illustration of what the relationship should be between a man, and his soul mate, or wife, and also how one "gains" immortality.

Remember how and why William Jefferson Clinton was busted? Remember his relationship and dealings with Monica Lewinski?

Was he a snake, demonstrating the demonic and satanic qualities of the "devil" in the "Garden of Eden?" Was there mutual love, respect, honor, sharing and caring there. Was there a lack of respect for the reproductive gifts, function, and process. And was there respect for the supposed completeness that a man has in his soul mate, his other half.

Wasn't it said or implied in the Bible that man was complete in himself – until the reproductive function became separate (through Evolution), and the intervention of the gods (and God)? And that to become "complete" again, the man "rejoined" himself to his other half, the woman?

Why was a "curse" put on the reproductive organs and function after the incident in Eden? Well, it may be because of the misuse of them – with the "snake."

The liar and seducer in Genesis told the truth – in a way. Jesus said the same thing!

You have to die to be born again, to have the eyes, specifically The Third Eye, opened. You "die" whenever you have a vision. You imitate that state. Concomitantly, you will gain discerning intelligence, the ability to reason, think, and judge, make logical and rational decisions, to become self-aware, and have Universal Consciousness. At some level it remains with you.

Actually, man has always maintained immortality – with conditions. The Holy Qur'an tells you specifically what some of those conditions are: See 39:42, 6:60, and 2:38.

When trying to figure out what the Bible means relating to the snake and Adam/Eve encounter, try this: substitute the word caress for the word bruise. Maybe the encounter was not about "eating" apples.

83

And to be born again, or "dying" means what? Change! This change or improvement gives one *discriminating* intelligence and knowledge. You analyze and make comparisons! You examine the up/down (or alternating) relationships, cycles, cause/ effect, action/reaction, man/woman, east/west, north/south, light/ darkness, and color/colorless aspects. You learn to connect the dots. You learn inductive and deductive reasoning! You also learn inference, subtlety, shades, tones, etc.

Eve and "the serpent" broke the covenant between soul mates. The matter involved reproduction. That's why it is said that "her punishment" related to her future reproduction. Also, Adam and Eve were looking backwards, (not forward) backsliding (like snakes). Maybe they were maintaining or opening their Third Eye – giving them the knowledge that they are immortal, somewhat analogous to the snake. It sheds its skin, JUST LIKE WE SHED OUR BODIES, and (we) live "forever!"

Also, what is the meaning of the name Eve? And does intimacy, complementation, mutual assistance, sharing and caring, love and support between the man and woman, as soul mates enable them to LIVE FOREVER? (Note: "Eve" means "life.")

The Creator(s) of man selected those who had demonstrated a certain growth, development, and other characteristics which identified them as Children of God, or "Adam." Were they hybrids of the Creator Beings?

The others humans were called the Children of Men. This is why Jesus, who is the reincarnation of Adam, (and Melchezidek, Joseph, Enoch, et.al.) is called the Son of Man, AND the Son of God. See? *We* are all Sons and Daughters of God and Man!

Genesis indicates that man was created by very advanced be- ings, (gods) and/or God! He initially "evolved!" First, "Adam" was androgynous, complete in himself, maybe self-fertilizing. Then, he evolved, or the Creator Beings operated on him, taking the cells from the marrow of "his rib" to create (clone) his sexual complement. I.E., reproduction began to be through fertilization from without, as we have in higher life forms.

Any discussion about the evolution of mankind on earth must consider several different things. Apparently different waves of beings incarnated on the earth at different times. There were the original inhabitants. They looked in many respects like some of the people we think of as Negroid peoples, i.e., the peoples of the Pacific regions, and in ancient times, (what we now think of as) the New World. You will also find traces of them in other places, in Asia and in Europe.

(WHO'S YOUR DADDY?)

Then, there was a change after the time of "Noah," perhaps millions of years ago. For then, only the "Blacks" and the "Reds-Browns" existed, according to the Bible. So, Noah's entourage, his family, and "posse" consisted of these types.

Remember, the "Reds," or Red-Browns were the "Adames," The Children of God. Were they genetically engineered from the "Blacks," and representing those who learned their lessons about certain practices, ideas, and conduct - and thereby moved on to the next progression of consciousness?

ALL MEN WERE CREATED EQUAL!

So, how did you get the other "races?" Well, we recently witnessed and *saw* an individual in the process of turning "white:" None other than the famous Pop Star, Michael Jackson. And from the Bible, we know about people turning white – the lepers! We know about Albinism.

The gods and God intervene in creation, in all our lives, to NORMALIZE, adapt, and integrate NEW creation into the preexisting creation. And they make MUTATIONS compatible to the earth's environment – as much as possible. And whatever Christ (gods) and God make (compatible) is good!

So, the waves of incarnations that make up the various so-called race groups, the 5 races, started millions of years ago, after the time of "Noah," and when mankind dispersed into the then CHANGING earth, into the cold regions, into the temperate regions – for the plates holding, maintaining, and shifting the continents and the seas operated, first separating us, then bringing us together, and eventually creating our current conditions.

(WHO'S YOUR DADDY?)

Later, there were colonies of hybrid Red-Brown Men (together with "Blacks" and others). They were the pyramid builders, and the creators of culture, art, tools, technology, and learning. The leaders considered themselves to be gods, and/or descended from the gods (or God). Some had a special knowledge, wisdom, understanding, and skill that we now call "Serpent Power!"

Some were Pharaohs of Egypt. Nebuchadnezzar, for example, and the others who had a legitimate claim to rule by Divine Right - by virtue of their linage, knowledge, wisdom, character, and nobility fall into this group.

Thomas Jefferson (Jacob), of the Bible, and others "showed" this ability. They showed that they "had a Divine Right to Rule" during their administrations or regimes. And nature and God agreed, and blessed their endeavors beyond imagination. Con- sider how Thomas Jefferson helped enable the 13 Colonies into the United States. Then, his efforts enabled what came to be 8 more (1. Kentucky, 2. West Virginia, 3. Illinois, 4. Indiana, 5. Wisconsin, 6. Michigan, 7. partly Minnesota, 8. Ohio).

Then, the Louisiana Purchase gave us 1. The rest of Minnesota, and all or parts of 15 other States, including: 2. Montana, 3. Wyoming, 4. Colorado, 5. Oklahoma, 6. Arkansas, 7. Louisiana, 8. Kansas, 9. Missouri, 10. Iowa, 11. Nebraska, 12. South Dakota, 13. North Dakota, 14. Texas, and 15. New Mexico.

So, $13 + 8 + 15 = 36$. This is the number of States Jefferson helped to bring into being. But he also sent Lewis and Clark to explore the land from Missouri to Oregon and the Pacific Ocean, thereby paving the way for the eventual acquisition of the other 14 States!

It does not appear that George Washington or John Adams had this divine blessing on their administrations. Did they have a Divine Right to rule?

Consider also: Jefferson enabled his two succeeding presidents, Madison and Monroe. Both had TWO terms. To accentuate the significance of Jefferson, both successors are named "James," are Democratic-Republicans, Virginians, and Monroe died on July 4th, just as Jefferson and John Adams had done in 1826. This highlights the importance of The Declaration, for its Jubilee Year is July 4, 1826. The lives of Sons of God versus Sons of Men show why there is a disparity of influence and capability.

In likeness, I am like Omar, the Third Progression, called the Second Caliph. For he is like Thomas Jefferson and Jacob, wily, smart, learned, fair, just, implementing and rewarding by merit – a noble Son of God!

I am like Alexander the Great, but he was very, very young. However, he knew he was a Son of God, a previous Egyptian, and in the image of Akenaten. Was Alexander not Alexander the Third?

He was acknowledged Pharaoh – and god, and appropriately interred in Memphis and then Alexandria. Alexander made many mistakes. He was God's hammer, but too young, too impatient. However, the pattern was correct. He would rule ALL the world – through Greek and Roman ideas, ideals, and practices.

He was also a builder, an architect, like Solomon. And is not King Solomon the Third Progression, but older, wiser here, (also) a lover of horses, a noble king?

Did not Thomas Jefferson build first, Greece and Rome, in the architecture of Monticello, The Virginia State House, the University of Virginia, and additions to the Washington DC Whitehouse?

And within, is this not the PATTERN of Israel? Aren't the rightful 42 Presidents PATTERNED like the 42 Patriarchs, and the 42 Provinces of Egypt?

Is it true: We shall build a Successor Temple of Solomon, overlooking a place like beautiful Pine Lake in University Park?

I am in image like Akhenaton – because there is no God but God! And I know WE come from the environment, substance, and vibration of the Sun, and when we regain our Unity, we MERGE *back* into the Sun!

Then, the Universe rejoices, it gently rains, and the music of the spheres is heard!

Therefore we are reddish-brown, noble, fearless, warriors, statesmen, impatient, fiery, with integrity – and Sons of God!

Eve was seduced by a snake. So, are some of our ancestors reptiles? Certainly, some lie, cheat, steal, kill, and destroy. And maybe snakes have become a part of our heritage, our lineage.

Remember my lineage? My father, Samuel is the seed of Mary and John. I am the seed of Ruby and Samuel.

So, I am Jimmy (because we come as a thief). I am James (Jacob), Joseph (Youssef), and Christ. That is just as it was with Jesus, the Messiah, see? In Luke, the lineage is given like this:

Jacob (Jimmy, James)
Joseph (Youssef)
Jesus (The Son of Man)
Christ (The Son of God)

OK, But Are People Like Snakes?

87

14 UFO'S? WHAT YOU TALKING ABOUT, WILLIS?

In visions, *in visions*, folks, I have seen UFO's! And I once (in vision) saw the inhabitants on the UFO. The inhabitants looked to me like maybe, Puerto Ricans – or somewhat like Barrack Obama, Minister Louis Farrakhan, maybe Malcom X. The two guys styled their hair about exactly like Farrakhan's. The skin was reddish-orange-brown.

They were asking me to come on up, to board their ship! I was asking them to come on down, and join me. I said to myself, then them, "If my two daughters were here, you wouldn't be able to get your butts *down here* fast enough!"

There were at least two other persons "associated" with the space vehicle. They were very "African," with very close cut hair. And they were very dark complexioned. And I knew that they were my long ago (lost?) ancestors, or relatives. And there was extremely great love and affection between me and my very "African" kinsmen and brothers.

On occasion, when I had these visions about UFO's, it would seem so real that I would think: "Aha! Finally, I see them in my conscious state, when previously, I have only seen them in dreams or visions!" I think I almost always saw them with Mother, Tonya, Runako, and sometimes Gloria and Noah present.

Are these associated with the gods, and the God who created us? Do they give us technology, assistance, and guidance? Do they interfere with the Inter-continental Ballistic Missile Systems on occasion, to show that they will not allow a nuclear war? Just wondering.

14.1 Do You See With Your Third Eye?

In Yoga, we activate the Third Eye, maintain Serpent Power, and see visions, and Astral Travel. We know that light travels in waves and particles. Does our hair, skin, pituitary, pineal, thyroid, parathyroids, kidneys, liver, heart, and other organs sense data (information) from our God and the gods that is converted into useful information by our brains?

Is one type of receptors better in conducting this information than others? Would the transmission be best between the reddish-brown types with the hair that is like light (wavy, and like particles) – and hair like wool, as white as snow, like "Christ" and God?

Example of use of the Third Eye: In an important vision in the early 1990's, Cathy Costner and I were together in Japan- and very "open" to each other. I said to her, "Thanks so much for meeting with me." We were both so golden brown, reddish-orange. Then, I saw a map of Asia and Europe. My eyes moved from east to west, stopping in Great Britain or Ireland. I believe the path followed a series of incarnations I have had: in Asia, Russia, Western Europe, and Great Britain. Finally, I saw rockets falling down on Great Britain! I called them "missiles," pronounced the British way.

14.2 Third Progression? What's That?

By "Third Progression," I mean the third guy: It would be 1. Abraham, 2. Isaac, 3. *Jacob*. Or , 1. Prophet Muhammad, 2. Caliph Abu Baker, 3. *Caliph Omar*. Or, 1. Jesse 2. King David, and 3. *King Solomon*. Or, 1. George Washington, 2. John Adams, and 3. *Thomas Jefferson*. See? Jesse is Patriarch #13 (also called a #4), a "transition, or the beginning of a new cycle. "31" or "40" would be a "4," or change.

Even certain qualities with Alexander qualify: See? He is *Alexander III* (The Third), etc.

I am the *third child*, a Gemini (the *third sign*) - and I have been able to access certain information about my *Third Progression* incarnations as *Thomas Jefferson* and *Jacob*.

14.3 Did Einstein Have A Lot of Bad Hair Days?

Well, you know how Albert Einstein's hair looked. You know how *energy* in light travels: in waves and particles! Could it be that Einstein picked up on vibrations, data, information, knowledge – transmitted to him, in part, through such sensory perception and receptors? Then, of course, the information is fed to the brain, for translation.

See, our hair(s) act as sensory devices – all over our body! This happens all over the animal kingdom, in worms, mammals, reptiles, fish, birds, etc.

So, is our "strength" partly in our hair, like in the story of Samson and Delilah? See the Tarot Card, #8, Strength, for a clue.

How is it that I see pictures, beings, things, in the dream state, or in visions? Well, we know that the Third Eye is the organ of sight for The Children of God who **have re-acquired** Serpent Power.

How is it that I can sometimes *hear* words, in the Meditation State? For, when I asked, Is Prophet Muhammad the reincarnation of Moses?" –

The Voice said, "Of Course!"

How did I *hear* the sound of **The Voice**, which "called" me (the Three Times, just like Samuel) to "the Ministry" in 1994? "

Who are the beings, or what is the force that answered my specific **questions, in a Meditation State**, using the format of the Yes/No option, and then selecting the appropriate response?

For, when I asked if I was the reincarnation of King David (in February, 2002), **"They"** said (selected) "No."

When I asked if I was the reincarnation of Thomas Jefferson (on 8/4/199), **They** said (selected) "Yes."

When I asked if Thomas Jefferson was the reincarnation (on 2/23/2002) of Jacob, **they** said (selected) "Yes."

When I asked if I am the reincarnation of King Solomon, (in February, 2002), **They** gave me an answer, but there was *too much light* coming through the window of my bedroom! So, I could not see what the answer (selection) was!

Swell! Is that *their* idea of a joke? He, he! ha-ha! See, The Third Eye functions best (and only) in relative DARKNESS – if you want to see pictures or graphic presentations!

And now, (since then) **"They"** won't tell me (or show me). Or, I cannot perceive **THEIR** answer. Such is the nature of our quest, our experimentation, and our journey. It is like the Sphinx: so many questions. (Sometimes it seems like) too few answers!

Do the Original Inhabitants of the earth, the so-called Negroids, pick up on certain information because their hair is conducive to the widest *vibrations* of the spectrum of light, or beyond? For their hair(s), ("hair like wool, as white as snow") and *other receptors* were sufficient in antiquity, during our descent into matter for good communication with our Father, God – and the gods! For, their hair is wavy, and like particles – like light!

Ok, the "white like snow" only applies when they get older, much older! Is Melanin, or color pigment, a conductor, receptor, or transmitter of energy? Remember E= MC (squared)?

90

14.4 What Time Is It?

Daniel 2:43 says, 2:43 And whereas thou sawest iron mixed with miry clay, they shall mingle themselves with the seed of men: but they shall not cleave one to another, even as iron is not mixed with clay (for they are intellectually challenged, without real knowledge, wisdom, and understanding- except for a few of them. And the few could not get through to the ignorant many. So we gave them a Civil War, World War I and World War II, and many more wars. But they still don't get it!)

2:44 And in the days (of the Eighth World Power) of these kings shall the God of heaven set up a kingdom, which shall never be destroyed: and the kingdom shall not be left to other people, [but] it shall break in pieces and consume all these kingdoms, and it shall stand for ever.

Finally, let us remember our contemporary saints, like Gwendolyn Brooks, and the numerous heroes of our era, like Marcus Garvey, Kwame Nkrumah, Sekou Toure, Gamal Abdul Nasser, Harold Washington, Patrice Lumumba, and Julius Nyerere.

Let's remember and honor our mighty men and heroes of ancient Egypt, Israel, Asia, Europe, Africa, and the New World!

And we have to remember where we came from. I believe the original humans looked like the individuals I saw "in-vision" on the UFO, who were with the other two red-brown types. Facially, they looked like many of the individuals currently in West Africa, and in the Americas. But some of the physiology (like the legs, for example) have greatly improved.

The "Adames" were the men of "red earth," and apparently were a later "creation," or evolution. They were red-brown, and looked like the ancient Egyptians. The Meshwaki, (The People of Red Earth, or Fox Indians) of Tama, Iowa, are at least symbolically one of "our" ancestors, for my son appeared to me as a beautiful red fox (in a vision).

But I have been in the Caucasus (in the beginning), and some roots are in "Middletown," Nigeria. And I was in Japan in 1637 when we expelled the Christians, and at other times. And I have been Chinese in ancient times.

I have seen the African types when they appeared to be about 10 feet tall (in vision). And I have been in the Americas when there was the coming of a glacier, or an Ice Age.

You cannot judge a book by its cover.

I am you. You are me. You and I are one.

WHO'S YOUR DADDY?

15 WHEN GOD LOVES YOU, HE WON'T GIVE YOU WHAT YOU WANT

When God loves you
He won't give you what you want.

He gives you Samuel
To idolize, love, and adore.
But "Sam" is a father, you do not know.
He gives a mother-to know,
And teach what *you* need to know.
Then, you take
God as your real father.

He gives you very few friends.
So, you value all the friendships you've ever had.
Once I had a friend- a good friend, an older guy.
And we planned to go fishing soon,
And not just work on cars.

So, God killed him.
And afterwards,
I took God as my friend.

Once I had a son, Jimmy Jr.
But because of my youthful ignorance,
He went back to heaven.

And God gave us a perfect
Daughter, Tonya,
So I could learn to love,
Understand, and appreciate women,
And not just sons.

And He gave us Runako,
So I could learn to
Love more,
And understand
That it is not just "Family First,"
As life is with Tonya,
But that the whole world is mine,
And the world is my family.

Then, God gave us Noah,
Because if you keep on living,
You have to grow up someday,
And assume full and total responsibility-for everything.
(And a man has to have a son.)
And know who you are and
Where you came from.
And you have to do
What you were born for,
This time.

And Noah teaches
All about *love-and-adoration* of sons,
Karma, peoples, cultures,
Patience, and tolerance.

But Noah is not perfect,
In the same way as Tonya and Runako,
But he teaches how to
Have perfect love.

And God gave our friend, Margaret,
To teach about relations/Muhammad's wives,
And that love really is blind
If she is good, beautiful, kind, and sexy.
And that when you try to help others,
You help yourself more than
You help them.

Then there is you.
And you teach and confirm that eventually,
A dream comes true.
The male body naturally manufactures "Viagra."
A man will know it when he meets Ms. Right.
Rebirth takes many forms.
Men need women as an inseparable part of themselves
When they do great things.

And if you love someone:

Tell them,
Show it,

Commit,
And only good will come of it.

And when God loves you,
He won't always give you what you want.
But, He gives you what you need.

16 I AM JUST LIKE YOU

I am very, very African.
Therefore, I can
Afford to reach out,
And be Chinese.

I saw myself as Chinese, in a beige suit.
And I did Martial Arts,
As Chinese.

I can throw a board right through your chest.
And I did.
I am... "a multitude of people"..."as (numerous) as
The dust of the earth."*
And I am just as Chinese, as any Chinese,
Because my soul
Is Chinese.

I am just as Japanese as
Any Japanese,
Because I (am a) Japanese soldier in 1637,
When we expelled the Christians,
Even though
I am Christian.

I was a great lover,
And my offspring are the proof.

I practiced yoga
Since 1971
(Even as a Muslim.)

And I saw Shaheen
In this life, and that life.
I love the Taj Mahal, even though it is a burial place.
Gandhi is one of my 7 M's (models),
Who is more Indian than I?

I am very Slavic, Northern European,
I lived in that swath of land
From Japan
To the British Isles.

I am just as Russian As Russia.
I conversed with Brezhnev,
Though we never met.

(I saw this:) "Russia" may destroy us
If NMD** proceeds,
And if we don't repent.

I am just as Jewish as any Jew,
For I am father of 12 boys, widely known as Jews.

I am very, very African.
As Jacob,
I died in Africa,@
Was buried in Palestine,
Can access some memory
Of that life.

I am Jefferson,
American,
Meshwaki (Fox)
Nigerian (from Jos)
French,
Christian, Muslim:

You are all my beautiful children.

God doesn't really care about
Your culture/ethnicity,
We care about you.

(I.E.), I am very, very African,
A Son of God,
And friend of God,
Your people;
I am
Just like you.

See Genesis 28:3, 14.
@ Egypt, Africa
**NMD = National Missile Defense

17 WHY WOMEN WANT MUSLIM MEN

We are family (first):

Which means
We love God (Allah):
Our Women,
Children,
Moses/Muhammad,
Jesus,
Justice, freedom, liberty,
Truth, and
Love.

We protect our family,
We are on the rise,

And Moses/Muhammad said,
As a religion of truth, Islam shall ... "prevail over
All other religions."*

And WE will make it happen.

Try a Muslim man,
And
See.

Note: See Chapter 48:28 (Surah Al-Fath/ The Victory)

18 WE WILL USE YOUR BODY

We will use your body
To reach your
Mind &
Soul.

We will
Renew &
Energize mind,
Body, &
Soul.

And ALL of
You
Will become
Becoming.

19 WE ARE THE PEOPLE'S POET

We are the People's Poet,

Advocate,

& Champion

Because
God really does love you.

And

We are

The People!

20 I AM

I am

A Muslim,

A Yogi,

A Pan-Islamist,

An American,

A Pan-Africanist,

An African Nationalist,

An African American,

Jewish, Christian, and Muslim.

I have integrity (thanks to God).

I am a thinker,

A worker, a father,

A Son of God!

Therefore,

I am.

21 TO BATTLE

When we stood toe to toe
I clobbered your beastly lie
And sent you gasping, fleeing.

I armed myself with truth,
And power from on high,
Did collar,
Flim-flam you,
You devilish dastardly liar:

I penetrate-transcended
Your lowly world of form,
(Cause I will power-form),
And weld the primal source.

When we give tit for tat,
I'll always send you fleeing!

Commentary: I composed the above selection as a result of a vision (from sometime in the early seventies) where I attacked a bearded, beastly looking Caucasian who somehow advanced toward me, threatening me. I hit him with the symbol of Aquarius, and defeated him!

22 THE TORCH HAS BEEN PASSED TO THE GENERATION OF THE CHILDREN OF GOD

Let the call go forth: to all Americans, to all nations, and to all people:

The torch has passed to the generation of the Children of God. And we will implement the *real* New World Order. And the culture of our New Millennium shall be that of sharing, caring, and unity with God.

And all God's children will have liberty, peace and security.

And the nations "…shall beat their swords into plowshares, and their spears into pruning hooks: nation shall not lift up sword against nation, neither shall they learn war anymore."*

The covenant that began 226 years ago with the Declaration of Independence has expired. America had its 42 legitimate presidents that mirror the 42 Prophet-Kings, Philosopher Priests of ancient Israel, starting with Abraham**, because the USA is most analogous to ancient Israel than the Zionist entity now in the Middle East.

U.S. identification with ancient Israel is deep. The third president of the United States, Thomas Jefferson, is Jacob, father of the 12 boys whose children became known as Israel.

Just as ancient Israel failed to live up to its agreement, so has America. And so 911 happened, in part, because the covenant has run out. And 911 is a taste of America's future: war, insecurity, famine (recession), and lack of freedom.

But today, God will "…set up a Kingdom, which shall never be destroyed: and the Kingdom shall not be left to other people, but it shall break in pieces and consume all (the previous) kingdoms, and it shall stand forever."***

We start by drawing up a New Covenant. We will have a New Republic, a new nation- that you can be proud to support. Together, we will implement Jubilee Worldwide, and we will wipe away all debt, for all peoples and all countries. We will implement sweeping amnesty, wherever possible. We may lower the voting age to sixteen. We will reinstitute sovereignty in the individual, and in the family. We will liberate women, and restore men to their rightful place. We will decriminalize that which is not criminal. We will privatize, democratize, and provide peace and security for all our citizens. We will organize block-by-block, as necessary. We will live by the Golden Rule. And we will usher in the real New World Order.

We will govern by the Law of Love, and the Rule of Law, and not satanic double standards, racism, oppression, and tyranny, as is now the case in the USA and elsewhere.

To those who oppose Jubilee and our other just and righteous measures: You will let my people go!

To: Americans: I respectfully assume my responsibility to tell you the truth. The USA is Babylon the Great, head of the Seventh and Eighth World Power. There is good America and bad America mixed in together. To support the bad policies of the current USA government is to support the devil. And if you support them, you will have The Mark of The Beast, and you will go to hell.

America, America. You have created the possibility of Heaven-On-Earth for many people. But you have created a living hell for far too many.

But today, we will have a rebirth. And God will bless our good with brotherhood, from sea to shining sea. And leadership shall be in caring and sharing, and not in exploitation and domination.

To African Americans: God has answered your prayer for freedom, justice, and equality-if you will be God's chosen. You are a beautiful rainbow of colors, and you are a beautiful people: You are *not* a minority, because I am Jacob, and *all peoples of the world are my children*, according to scripture. *I am African American*, and I am one of you.

Minorities are devils on earth, in rebellion against God. We are *with* God, and we will bind *minorities* for 1000 years.

On behalf of all good Caucasians, Africans, and others, past and present, I apologize for slavery, colonialism, and imperialism, the real Axis of Evil.

And this Axis of Evil created conditions where 1 billion of God's children exist on about $1 per day, and another 2 billion, about $3 per day, and they lie, cheat, steal, destroy, and deny accountability and responsibility for their crimes against God and man.

104

What goes around comes around. He who leads into captivity, shall go into captivity. He who kills with the sword, shall be killed with the sword. That is the law of action/reaction, cause and effect.

To Africa and Africans: You are my firstborn. And you are my first love; you are my sweetheart. My roots are in "Middletown," Nigeria. And I have seen tropical African vegetation, streams, and even a Totem Pole-when I look within myself.

Africa must unite! Africa must do it now! And join with me as God's dear Chosen.

To Native Americans and other native peoples who have had genocide, land theft, and other unjust acts committed against you: It is not possible to apologize for genocide and other unjust measures committed against you. But, I can assure you that God will right the wrongs that have been heaped upon you.

And I can tell you that I was here thousands of years ago, when there was an Ice Age on this North American continent. And I have seen scenes of Atlantis, in dreams or visions. And I am Meshwaki, or Fox Indian, and I am one of you. My son once appeared to me as a beautiful, red fox. So, I am Fox, or Meshwaki. And we shall overcome!

To Russia and China: I am just as Russian as you are. I am just as Chinese as any Chinese. My best friend is Russian, with the most beautiful eyes that show what a blend of Russia and China can be. The earth is the Lord's, and the goodness thereof. Therefore, we will share our resources, talents, and skills with you. We will beat our swords into plowshares, and our spears into pruning hooks, and we shall study war no more-because all of us are one people, under God, with liberty and justice for all!

To Pakistan and India: What do you think Gandhi would think of your confrontation over Kashmir? And India, what should a *man* do if his wife is determined to get a divorce from him? Look, the nation-state is a bad idea anyway. It's a condition that keeps people apart, not one that brings them together. What nation-state on earth is righteous, just, truly democratic, and truly a good neighbor?

I am an American Muslim, and I practiced yoga since 1971. So I have a Muslim heritage and a Hindu heritage, and I am a part of India and Pakistan.

I am an African American, and I knew my great grandmother. And this country, the USA enslaved my very own great grandmother. And this country practiced genocide, and they killed my Native American ancestors, the Meshwaki and the Sauk "Indians," and they came close to extinction. And they enslaved and committed unspeakable crimes against my African ancestors. And this country has committed, and does commit numerous crimes against other peoples of this earth because they don't treat others like they want to be treated, and they practice a double standard. And I will forgive them!

And India and Pakistan must forgive each other and share a relationship with Kashmir, and together confront the real enemy of God and man on earth. And Kashmir has a right to self-determination. But, the nation-state is something we will do away with (in its present form) anyway.

To Muslims worldwide: Cease and desist! Don't attack the U.S.A. I am Jacob/Thomas Jefferson, father of the 12 tribes of Israel. I am one of you. Together, we can take care of the problem of America. We will have a new government, truly of the people and by the people, and not this tyranny, now on the necks of U.S. citizens, and at the throats of other peoples of the world.

We are here to wrap up the cycle of Judaism, which includes ancient Judaism, Christianity, and Islam. They are all basically the same-part of the evolution of Judaism. And real Muslims will now, today, include within Islam holidays like Passover, Hanukkah, Christmas, and Easter, so that "Islam will prevail over all other religions." ****

To the "Jews" of the State of Israel: I am Jacob, father of the 12 tribes. Who is more Jewish than I?

The brutal onslaught against my people, the Palestinians, shows the whole world that the perpetrators are ignorant and brutal people. They are not Jews. A Jew is just, fair and good. A Jew is helpful and beneficial to mankind. A Jew is not an oppressor and a warmonger. The rulers of the Zionist state cannot be Jews. Only devils do what they are doing.

There are three reasons that 911 happened: Israel, oil, and Israel. There *were* three reasons for the war against Iraq: Israel, oil, and Israel. And the war was an immoral and unjust war-and that's why it was unsuccessful, and is unresolved. **911 is a result** of the war against Iraq.

Israel is the problem in the Middle East. We must remove or ameliorate the problem.

If you are a real Jew you know what Daniel 9:24-27 says: "70 weeks (490 years) are determined upon thy people and upon thy holy city, to **finish the transgression, and to make an end of sins, and to make reconciliation for iniquity,** and to bring in everlasting righteousness, and seal up the vision and the prophecy, and to anoint the most Holy. Know therefore and understand that from the going forth of the commandment to restore and build Jerusalem (457 BC) unto Messiah, the prince shall be 7 weeks, and threescore and 2 weeks: the street shall be built again, and the wall, even in troublous times. And after threescore and 2-weeks shall Messiah be cut off, but not for himself…And he shall confirm the covenant with many for one week (7-years), and in the mist of the week, he shall cause the sacrifice and the oblation to cease, and from the overspreading of abominations, he shall make it desolate…."

490 years minus 457 BC is 34 AD, the time when bad Jews killed the Apostle Steven, **and the covenant with ancient Israel ended.**

Bad Jews were full of sin, and they killed the prophets.

Christians believe that they killed the Messiah, Jesus. That's why they got expelled from Palestine. And the Dispensation (Mission, or Torch) was given, in-turn to the Christians, and then to the Muslims.

The Prophet Muhammad is Moses, reincarnated again, in 570 AD My Jewish blood, through my offspring, including the Ten Lost Tribes, runs in the veins of all the peoples of the world. There is no such person as a Gentile who is different from a Jew. We are all the same: All Jews. Chairman Arafat is as much a Jew as any Jew-biologically. The Palestinians are just as Jewish as anybody. The Israel-Palestinian issue shows how dangerous ignorance and lies are. To say that the state of Israel has a right to exist is an extreme and blasphemous lie. And the result is the extreme of suicide bombing-to explode that extreme lie!

The last time I counted, Bush told Sharon 8 times to get out of the West Bank. Sharon told Bush to go pound sand. Bush is impotent in the face of Israel. It's a case of wag the dog. And the supposed elected officials of US citizens show that they are in the pocket of the lobbyists for Israel.

Why is Bush impotent in the face of Israel and Sharon? Does Sharon dangle pretzels in Bush's face, and frighten him?

Bush is an illegitimate, wannabe president, who chokes on a pretzel, and who has no real power when he deals with the Zionist entity. As long as this illegitimate tyrant sits on the seat of Babylon, the Great, you will have war, famine, and desolation.

US citizens must replace a Congress that represents the illegitimate state of Israel. If they want to represent the Zionist entity, let them go there and get elected by bad Jews. Real Jews will overcome the impostors. And Real Jews accept Jesus as Messiah, and Moses/ Muhammad as Messenger of Allah.

God's chosen, the Real Nation of Israel, are those scattered through-out the earth among the various points to which the lost tribes were scattered, and who make choices to join with us in the Spiritual Revolution and The Second Coming, and to complete the cycle of Judaism (which includes ancient Judaism, Christianity, and Islam.)

So America needs elected representatives that represent America, not the illegitimate state of Israel.

Be a real Jew: accept Jesus as Messiah; accept Moses/Muhammad as Messenger of Allah. And help your fellow Jews (the Arabs), by sharing resources, talents, skills, and bringing the truth to them!

To the media, TV, Cable, and to the entertainment business: There is some good in you. But too much of what you produce has too much violence, sex, and decadence. You are too superficial, and you are too trivial. Too little of what you say and do is true, or correct. Far too much of your products are not fit for human consumption. You are a pollution on the earth. And that *will* change.

To all nations and peoples. I am your friend and your brother. I will always be just and fair to you. **And to those who are Antichrist, and oppose our good work, and pick a fight with us: we will try to erase you and all memory of you from the universe!**

We must phase out secret, subversive, and clandestine agencies that destabilize and kill people and nations, like the US and French CIA, Israeli Mossad, and the KGB. *The best government is the least government, and accountable government.* When we are self-regulating, the need for any police force is minimal. And we will be so healthy, in all respects, that police, doctors, and medicine will henceforth take on new and different missions.

I came here before, in 1743 (As Thomas Jefferson) to set the stage for the cleansing of the Sanctuary, (in 1844). And I came back again in *1944*, about 100 years after the cleansing of the Sanctuary, to make way for The Judgment to sit.

And I will gather you this Second Time, "…from Assyria, and Egypt, and from Pathros, and from Cush, and from Elam, and from Shinar, and from Hamath, and from the Islands of the sea." And "they shall not hurt nor destroy in all my holy mountain: for the earth will full of the knowledge of the Lord, as the waters cover the sea."*****

To all real Jews, Muslims, and Christians: We are here to seal you with The Seal of God. **And we reaffirm the law of God (that is, the Law of the Universe), handed down through Moses/ Muhammad: God is One, that is, the universe is Unity and interdependence. We live and have our being in God. We are all connected!**

Pork is forbidden. Homosexuality is an aberration, and against the laws of the universe. Moderation is often best in whatever you do.

To Moses/Muhammad, Jesus, our Brotherhood, our Elders, Wise Men, Shamen, priests, and good ones throughout the universe: We solicit and welcome your help. Together, with God, we shall overcome!

And to all mankind: All nations will have judges, as in the case of ancient Israel, when Moses led us; and our illustrious son, Samuel, led us; and also in the case when Moses was known as Muhammad, and that time he led us-right *into* the Promised Land.

We will beat our swords into plowshares, and our spears into pruning hooks, and we shall study war no more-because all of us *are* one people, under God, with liberty and justice for all.

And all judges will be of one accord, in Christ (i.e., in God). And we will serve God and man. And we will look back at the time of the silly barbarians, and those with the Mark of the Beast, and thank God for our real New World Order!

Youssef Khalim 5/29/02, Revised 9/7/2005

*Isaiah 2:4
**See Matthew 1:1-18, See The Resurrection of Noah
***Daniel 2:44
****
*****Isaiah 11:11, 11:9

23 I CALL MYSELF AFRICAN AMERICAN

I call myself African American because words have power-and meaning. The term "African American" best indicates my ancestral roots, heritage, and who I am today.

I am a son and heir to those coming out of Egypt (Africa) called Moses, Aaron, Joshua, and their kinsmen. I am an heir to the land, blood, might, glory, and culture of Egypt, Ethiopia, Libya, Nigeria, Morocco, and other *African* places.

Likewise, I am a son of the Meshwaki, the Sauk, and the various peoples of the Western World. And I am a son of the British, Irish, Slavs, and other European settlers of the Western World.

To call myself a color, like Black or White is highly superficial and flawed. I don't believe the Chinese call themselves Yellow. And when was the last time you heard them call themselves Mongoloid? Do Indians, Pakistanis, Puerto Ricans, Latinos and Bangladeshis call themselves Blacks, or Browns? Successful peoples realize that proper self-identification is a key to freedom, security, success, and happiness.

Historically, it was accepted that Africans and descendants of Africans should be called by the name indicating the *land* of their origin. The African Methodist Episcopal (AME) Church, founded in 1787, in Philadelphia, Pennsylvania, by a group led by 27-year old, Richard Allen, is an example of this recognition.

Africans in America were also called *People of Color,* and the *National Association for the Advancement of Colored People* (NAACP), founded on 2/12/1909, is an example of this recognition.

Concurrent to the times of the founding of the NAACP, and up to the present time, the term Negro is sometimes used. W. E. B. Du- Bois, Marcus Garvey, Martin Luther King, Jr., Malcolm X, John H. Johnson, and many others used this name for self-identification, and in organizations, and publications. Examples include:

1. W. E. B. DuBois used the term Negro, Black, and African almost interchangeably. To see an example of how he used these terms, read his book, *The Souls of Black Folk*, published in 1903.

2. *The Universal Negro Improvement Association (UNIA)*, was founded by Marcus Garvey; and by the early 1920's, the UNIA had established 700 branches in thirty-eight states.

3. Martin Luther King, Jr. often used the term *Negro,* as exemplified in his famous "I Have A Dream" speech of August 28, 1963.

4. Malcolm X sometimes used the term Negro, but often used the term, *so-called Negro*, indicating his realization of its inadequacy. In his later life, Malcolm often used some variation of the term "Afro-American."

5. Negro Digest, founded by John H. Johnson, in 1942, discontinued in 1951, and restarted again in 1961, is also a history of the use of the term, Negro. The publication was renamed *Black World* in 1970, reflecting the tenor of the times. By 1976, circulation dropped to 15,000 and the magazine was discontinued.

During the early 1960's, many African American leaders and the middle-class were promoting the name, Negro. Martin Luther King, Jr. (SCLC), A. Philip Randolph (Union leader), Ralph Bunch (United Nations), James Farmer (CORE), Roy Wilkins (NAACP), and Johnson Publications are examples of this group. However, various individuals simultaneously used the names Afro-American, African-American, and Black at various times.

Many in the Civil Rights Movement became impatient over the progress toward voting rights, and over discrimination in housing, employment, and various other areas. Some groups and individuals searched for more effective ways to empower African Americans, and solve many of their problems. Stokley Carmichael, a leader of The Student Nonviolent Coordinating Committee (SNCC), and other like-minded individuals therefore called together a *Black Power* Conference in 1966. (Stokley was very young at this time.)

These more aggressive forces started promoting the term *Black*, and it began to be promoted in songs, literature, culture, government, and politics.

In the sixties and seventies, many of us made attempts at indicating that we are an African people. We started spelling the name, *Afrikan*, with a "k," instead of "c" to indicate that we reclaimed and embraced African history, culture, and roots. In 1971, I started an organization called United Afrikans For One Motherland, International (UFOMI), with Ruwa Chiri (of Zimbabwe), and others, to promote a Pan-African agenda.

The vast majority of African Americans are some variation of brown, in appearance. Others are "yellow," reddish, or black. Some are indistinguishable from Caucasians, Asians, or other groups.

To call African Americans, *Black,* is not wise. It can be crippling- maybe that's why it was, and is promoted. There is no "Blackland" There is, however, the land of Africa. Names of identification, race, and ethnicity should be based on the *land* of one's origin, blood-lines, culture, heritage, and roots. To say that you are *Black* also says, *on some level*, that you came from nowhere. If you came from nowhere, how far can you go? To say that you came from nowhere sharply limits your imagination, creativity, sense-of-identity, aspirations, capabilities, and worldview. And to say that you came from nowhere is not true.

My perspective is limitless! The name, African American, indicates that I am a full member of the total fabric of American society; my ancestors are the original inhabitants of this land. My bloodlines and culture are also of Africa, Europe, and the world. Therefore, I am an integral and indispensable part of America, and the world.

The use of the name, African American, (without the hyphen) does *not* preclude the use of the terms Black, or Negro. It's just a more accurate name for where I came from, where I'm going, my ancestral roots, and heritage, and who I am today.

Good nation-building examples: Chinese, "Jews:" When African Americans and other groups get serious about growth, development, education, self-identity, and nation-building, they will look at the Chinese, Japanese, South Koreans, and look at the Europeans who call themselves Jews, for guidance and example. They certainly will not call themselves a color!

24 WE MAY LOWER THE VOTING AGE TO 16

History has shown that we incline to live up to expectations, and that Natural Development cannot long be denied.

In order to properly adjust our expectations, and align our system with the reality existing in nature, promote democracy and account-ability, and counter the existence of Taxation Without Representation, the voting age shall be lowered to age sixteen. If demonstrated maturity of Natural Development is present, then, the individual may be allowed to vote at age fifteen. The adult age is still 21.

In further defense of this proposal, we offer the case of Mary, mother of Jesus, who, they tell us, became expecting at the age of fifteen, and delivered the Messiah at age sixteen.

When Jesus was 12-years old, he and his parents went to a feast in Jerusalem. When they left, he stayed behind, and was separated from them for four days, because he wanted to discuss religious, philosophical, and relevant issues with wise and learned men, and he was about the business of God. *Good people* are like Mary, and we are like Jesus.

After my grandmother, the midwife, cut the cord between my Mom and me, she and others cleaned me up. Then, I "raised my head up high and looked around the room. Side-to-side, I looked-all around the room. I lowered myself back down. Then, I did it again." And my Mom, grandmother, Aunt Hattie, and her husband (Uncle Will) witnessed this event. And they were astonished. So, I was born in Cleveland, Mississippi, near a farming community, on June 3, 1944.

At the age of 7, I used to clean, maintain the house, and do some cooking while the adults, or older people tilled or harvested the crops. I collected eggs from our own and other peoples' chickens. I also gathered foods such as berries, okra, pecans, pears, peaches, plums, melons, tomatoes, and persimmons for the family. And I fished, and helped take care of the family pets.

At about the age of nine and ten, I used to hire-out to till or harvest crops for other farmers. I would also gather firewood, chop down trees, plow the fields, run errands, operate a "trout-line" in the bayou, catch fish, edible turtles and frogs, and gather water from outdoor pumps.

At about the age of ten, I could carry a sack of cotton weighing well over 100 pounds. And I harvested corn, cotton, and other products.

At the age of eleven, (in Chicago) I changed my name from "Jimmie" to James, on my own, and without any consultation with anyone. Also, I operated a snowball wagon, and sold snowball cones.

And I earned money by doing odd jobs for relatives. At 12, I had a newspaper route on the West Side, and I delivered newspapers (at times) from about Racine Avenue to past Damen Avenue, near Roosevelt Road. I also maintained the house while my Mom worked. And I cooked full meals, and learned to use cookbooks.

During this time, I bought my own bike, and I commuted to our Newspaper Route office, on Racine, from as far away as Christiana Ave.

At the age of 14, I began working in a grocery store. First, I would just clean up and mop the floor, after store hours. Later, I did all the jobs at the store. And I bought all my own clothes, and also helped provide money for our family.

At fifteen and sixteen, I continued working at the grocery store, and I provided the money for all my High School needs, including commuting to and from school, (on Chicago's South Side) and class, band, and ROTC uniform fees.

During the time when I was 11-16, I was an excellent student. I was an Honor Student, and I read newspapers and magazines to stay informed on all events worth knowing about in the world. I also read books about politics, religion, and current events. At the age of 15-16, I was in ROTC, the High School Band, and I was on the Wrestling Team.

At the age of seventeen, I was so eager to be eighteen that I tried to put my age up to eighteen. At 17-18, I bought my own brand new car, and I bought two lots of land in Hawaii.

My older brother, and many other children had similar responsibilities in Mississippi and Chicago. So, I was well qualified to vote at age fourteen, and I'm sure that other children are qualified at a similar age (14-16).

I have watched young peoples' participation in events all over the world-for years. In some instances, their experiences are similar to mine because they sometimes take on significant responsibilities at young ages. Some are even soldiers in wars, in Liberia, Sierra Leone, Afghanistan, and elsewhere. In Palestine, brave and wonderful youth fight the tanks and gunships of the devil, with stones.

So, our bright and wonderful US youth, because of their ascendant positions, have a responsibility to assist their peers in other lands who are often literally under fire-by electing humane, moral, and responsible leaders here, and not those who betray America and side with oppressors and tyrants, and the enemies of God and man.

114

All youth throughout the world must show solidarity with other youth because it is the right thing to do. For, liberation will come-by the ballot, or the bullet.

And youth must make the decision to assume the responsibility to take up the ballot - to expand the rights of man, and to liberate, assist, and free man- kind-so we don't have to take up arms.

Youssef Khalim 6/8/02

Delegates to A New USA Constitutional Convention:

The most desirable qualifications Delegates to the USA Constitutional Convention will have are listed below. Attendance methods may include Conference Calls, Internet Logon, and/or physical presence.

1. Integrity-Is honest, truthful. Has inclination to tell the facts, and the truth.
2. Justice-Has a sense of justice, fairness, belief in The Golden Rule, and belief that Right Makes Might.
3. Courage-Has courage, and only fears not doing the right thing.
4. Goodness-Has belief in his/her own goodness, and in the actual or potential goodness of *all* mankind. Tries to have the right thoughts, words, and actions.
5. Logical, rational-Is sincere, thoughtful, factual, and scientific.
6. Practical, purposeful-Believes in practical application of beliefs and knowledge.
7. Belief in God-Believes in a higher form of existence, and the Spiritual (unseen) aspects of life.
8. Ages 16, and above-Note: We invite those with these qualifications to join with us.
9. Healthy-Is vigorous, energetic, and healthy of mind, body, and soul.
10. Resourceful, with initiative-Has energy, initiative, creativity, and imagination.
11. Respectful-Has respect for the rights, space, and person of others.
12. Responsible and accountable-Is responsible and accountable.

Youssef Khalim 7/30/02

25 MOTHER IS NOT DEAD

Luke 20:38 says, "For He (God) is not a God of the dead, but of the living: for all live in Him."

Matthew 22:31,32 says, "But as touching the resurrection of the dead, have ye not read that which was spoken unto you by God, saying, I am the God of Abraham, and the God of Isaac, and the God of Jacob? God is not the God of the dead, but of the living."

Matthew 9:23, says, "And when Jesus came into the ruler's house, and saw the minstrel and the people making a noise,

24) He said unto them, Give place: for the maid is not dead, but sleepeth. And they laughed him to scorn

25) But when the people were put forth, he went in, and took her by the hand, and the maid arose.

In Chapter 39:42, the Holy Qur'an says, "It is Allah Who takes away the souls at the time of their death, and those that die not, during their sleep. He keeps those souls for which He has ordained death and sends the rest back for a term appointed...."

In Chapter 2:28, it says, How can you disbelieve in Allah? Seeing that you were dead and He gave you life. Then He will give you death, then again will bring you to life, and then unto Him you will return."

Mother is NOT dead! She is resting, reviewing her life and earthly relations, and continuing with her growth and development, as she and God see fit! She grew out of her previous body! What can you expect? 84 years is a long time to be carrying around one body! And you know how it is: We always want to get the latest and the greatest!

Mother now has on her white robes, washed in the Blood of the Lamb! So, she must have some kind of body, and I believe she has a better body!

A case in point: I had to buy my 11 year-old son, Noah, a new *suit* and shoes to wear to this celebration, this event, because he is now 5 ft. tall, and he grew out of his old suit. Likewise, Mother will get a new body to *suit* her, now and in the future!

Mother is also very much alive in her 5 children, 30 grandchildren, 85 great grandchildren, and 36 great great-grandchildren!

And Mother will continue to be with us, in mind and spirit, wherever the bond of love, friendship, support, and caring and sharing exists.

So, we are here today to celebrate her life, hopes, dreams, and her wonderful legacy!

Mother was born over 84 years ago in Shaw, Mississippi! As I said, she has five living children. Fred, Jr., is no longer with us. But you know what? I saw Fred in a dream around about the time mother went into Holy Cross, and then into Little Company of Mary. And I got the feeling that his appearance and Dorothy's comments might indicate that something very serious was imminent.

Fred usually visits me 'round the time of his birthday. And he often visits me (in dreams) around the time of my birthday. So, Fred's visit was not in keeping with his usual routine.

A few weeks later I saw two dreams where Mother was much, much better! So, obviously this meant that she is better - where she is now!

I saw Mother for the last time, Monday night, about 10:00 PM! And I did some silent prayers and healing, and life energy exercises with her. And she distinctly called out my name a number of times, "Jimmy, Jimmy!"

You know Mother once had three Jimmy's in her house. I am Jimmy number-1, named after my great grandfather, James Shinault. Then, there is my *youngster* brother, James. And Mom was married to Jimmy Anderson, Ivory's father. She apparently was determined to get as much Jimmy as reasonably possible in her life.

I was usually around and available to help Mother, even from the time I was about 7-years old!

And Mother was there for me - always, for any available assistance, and for conversation, and moral and concrete support!

Did you ever feel that you had the perfect mother for you? Well, I feel and felt that way about Mother - and I told her so many times. I had just the right start in secular education, religious education, and moral teachings from her.

Mother was kind, generous, loving, supportive, and sharing. She was a giver - not a taker. Mother would often borrow money, to give to someone in need! Mother was not judgmental, and she respected her children's' space, privacy, freedom, and choices.

Mother, Fred, and I came to Chicago around Thanksgiving Day in 1955, right around the time Emmet Till was murdered, in Mississippi!

Mother always worked hard. She worked past her retirement age. Fred and I worked hard too, and we helped Mother. First, I sold Snowballs. Then, I had a Paper Route. Then, I worked in a grocery store, the Post Office.... You get my point! Fred and James' work situation was similar to mine.

117

Mother taught us to think for ourselves, be ourselves, believe in, and trust ourselves, be the best that we can be, develop and grow, tell the truth, have integrity and courage, and believe in a Higher Reality! Mother's decision to take Chemotherapy, and the way she fought and struggled for life, shows her fierce courage and determination - to the bitter end!

She taught me to never, ever give up! Try to learn all secular knowledge. But go to God for real knowledge, wisdom, and understanding. Mother was talking about reading, studying, and getting more education for herself - just a few months ago.

Mother taught me how to take care of my body, how to heal my body, respect my body. And she taught me that the body is The Temple of The Living God!

Mother taught me how to *think and be* positive, constructive, responsible, and helpful!

Mother taught me that all work is honorable, if you are an honorable person!

She taught me how to be silent, how to think the right thoughts, say the right and proper words, and take the right actions! She taught me to be very, very careful with my words. Once they escape your mouth, (she showed) you cannot call them back! Words can hurt! Words *can* kill! You don't believe me? Just look at some people, just look in some neighborhoods! So, learn this great lesson from my Momma!

Mother lived in our building on West Adams Street, from about 1971 through 1982. Then, she lived with us, on West Van Buren Street. Then, she lived with Fred, until he passed away.

Ruby Lee Watson's legacy will be that she always tried to help her children, grandchildren and great grandchildren - and she always tried to teach them right from wrong, and correct moral and spiritual values.

We, the sons and daughters of Ruby Lee Watson must be inspired here, today, to honor her life, and to build fitting and lasting monuments to her by:

1. Planting some gardens.
2. Starting a *Ruby Lee Robinson Hospital, and Healing and Cancer Research Institute.*
3. Starting our own schools, somewhat like Haki Madhubuti's Schools.
4. Opening some restaurants, because Ivory, Tonya, Dorothy and others *can,* and should do that!
5. Moving ahead with our own Illinois corporation, called *Sun Ra Communications, Inc.,* and using SCORE, city, state, and other resources to accomplish this.

6. And doing other things that show proper respect for Mother's life.

Mother is not dead. She is resting! And if and when we build a suitable environment of love and welcome, she and God might send her back - so we can share more love with her!

26 MY BORN AGAIN EXPERIENCE – VISIONS

6/18/1997: Vision at about 3:30 AM this morning, I had one of the top most vision experiences, similar to what occurred on 7/20/1980.

It was called (or I experienced) Being Born Again! There was much light (s): some seeming to come into me, soaking me,

And If I Had Not Been Righteous, there is the feeling that I would not have passed this test, but rather been destroyed by the power of the Light and Energy.

I saw many lamps, lit up and burning, very energetically! Lots of "sound, energy, wind."

26.1 The Lorraine Vision

"7-12-80: I Had this wonderful dream: She lived with her mother. Father was deceased. Father got her involved w/going to a night spot which played jazz. She still went there. Her mother was concerned that she had not gotten married. She had blond hair, around the edges at least. She had a deep tan. Light blue eyes. She took me in kiss as we necked and while I caressed her. I kissed her chest. She could not take much of this. I started to kiss intimately but she said, 'No, not that way.' I was ready to enter her, but there was a question of contraceptives. I awakened. Her chest was really brown with tanning. She had brown somewhat large freckles over parts of her body. And she was soft and smooth and desirable. She would have been Capricorn type."

Note: Questions were asked about the dream: "Was this past life? What is the name of the individual? How may this individual be contacted?"

The response, on or about 7-12-80:

"It is up to this individual to do the contacting in this case. The dream is a way to prepare for the contact when and if it is made and to allow you, as the entity involved in the contact to recognize the reaching out that should take place. There are, however, present life symbols layered upon that reality of the dream; the music symbolizing the spiritual roots of the culture of the heritage, and music as an outlet of creative spirit, an outlet under- stood across the varying cultures though rooted in one, a symbol of creativity, as a bridge between the various cultures with whom the entity is to deal."

120

26.2 Interpretation of the "Lorraine Vision"

The following is about the dream and a purported interpretation of it in July, 1980. I believe that I met the individual referenced to in the dream on about the same day of the dream. Her name was Lorraine.

Lorraine means "laurel," which is an evergreen. Your name, of course, means lily. As if to accentuate that, you sometimes wear a white flower-like ornament in your hair. I have previously mentioned the strong symbolisms showing qualities reflective of "Diana, moon goddess" in your personality profile.

But back to Lorraine: I created the attached poem reflective of her within the following week. I believe Lorraine would be called a redhead, and she had hazel eyes. She might, however, be called a platinum blond. Her father was not deceased, but he had given up on his aspirations and goals in life, and so it was like he had given up living. Lorraine did like jazz. She was very bright, and wise, generous, kind.

She did have freckles over her chest. But she was not very brown, as in the dream. Lorraine said that the dream might refer to a mutual friend of ours, who is blond (and has the Slavic surname, through marriage, of Sladek). Lorraine's eyes appeared green most of the time.

26.3 The Temptation of Jesus – Another Vision

We all know the story of Jesus being baptized by John, the Baptist, then fasting for 40 days and being tempted of "the devil."

The story of the temptation is in the 4th Chapter of Matthew:

1: Then was Jesus led up of the Spirit into the wilderness to be tempted of the devil.

2: And when he had fasted forty days and forty nights, he was afterward an hungered.

3: And when the tempter came to him, he said, If thou be the Son of God, command that these stones be made bread.

4: But he answered and said, It is written, Man shall not live by bread alone, but by every word that proceedeth out of the mouth of God.

5: Then the devil taketh him up into the holy city, and setteth him on a pinnacle of the temple,

6: And saith unto him, If thou be the Son of God, cast thyself down: for it is written, He shall give his angels charge concerning thee: and in their hands they shall bear thee up, lest at any time thou dash thy foot against a stone.

7: Jesus said unto him, It is written again, Thou shalt not tempt the Lord thy God.

8: Again, the devil taketh him up into an exceeding high mountain, and sheweth him all the kingdoms of the world, and the glory of them;

9: And saith unto him, All these things will I give thee, if thou wilt fall down and worship me.

10: Then saith Jesus unto him, Get thee hence, Satan: for it is written, Thou shalt worship the Lord thy God, and him only shalt thou serve.

11: Then the devil leaveth him, and, behold, angels came and ministered unto him.

26.4 Khalim's "Temptation" Vision

I had a similar experience in about 1971 or 1972. In fact, to me it kind of seemed like the same experience, *but with notable exceptions as to the temptation!*

It seems that I was lifted up high (but not into a mountain). The affect seemed, and seems just like being lifted, like Jesus "....up into an exceeding high mountain, and sheweth him all the kingdoms of the world, and the glory of them;" (Mathew 4:8).

But, alas, Elijah Muhammad (of The Nation of Islam) appeared to me and said (or somehow indicated) to me that he was "God."

I said to him (or thought), "He is too light-complexioned to be God!"

Commentary: I realize the above vision seems odd. It does, however have meaning, and useful symbolism to me.

27 THE USA STEALS CHILDREN – HOLDS THEM CAPTIVE

Former Illinois Governor, Jim Edgar, Charlene Necco, (of DCFS) Judge James Cerri, (of Will County Court, in Joliet, Illinois), and other lying, corrupt, degenerate thugs in Illinois (still) steal babies.

Yes, this is incredible! It is even more incredible when you know the people in Illinois who knew about this, starting with former U. S. Attorney, Jim Burns, the ACLU, and numerous other State, Civil Rights, and Non-profits. Below is a listing of those who received distribution of legal briefs concerning this matter.

See the distribution list below:

Then, see a copy of the related court filing, on about 7/24/1994, page 126.

(Distribution List):

TO:

1. U.S. Attorney James Burns
   Attn: Mike Peligan
   219 S. Dearborn St., 5th floor
   Chicago, Illinois 60604

2. ACLU- Roger Baldwin Foundation
   203 N. LaSalle St., Suite 1405
   Chicago, Illinois 60601

3. The Rev. Jesse L. Jackson, Sr.
   C/O Operation Push
   930 E. 50th Street
   Chicago, Illinois 60615

4. The Honorable Carol Mosely Braun
   Senator, United States Congress
   230 S. Dearborn St., Suite 3900
   Chicago, Illinois 60604

5. The Honorable Boutros Boutros-Ghali
   Secretary General, United Nations C/O
   UN Commission! Human Rights
   United Nations
   New York, N.Y. 10017

6. The Honorable Dr. Conrad Worrill
   C/O MILLION MAN MARCH Committee
   National Black United Front
   700 E. Oakwood Blvd.
   Chicago, 111.60653

7. The Honorable Minister Louis Farrakhan
   C/O MILLION MAN MARCH Committee
   Mosque Maryam
   7351 S. Stoney Island Ave.
   Chicago, Illinois 60620

8. The Honorable Rickey Hendon
   Senator, The State of Illinois
   538 N. Western Ave.
   Chicago, Illinois 60612

9. Mark Kadish
   Chicago Kent College of Law
   565 W. Adams St.
   Chicago, Illinois 60606

   10. Larry Yellen
       FOX WFLD TV
       205 N. Michigan Ave. Chicago,
       Illinois 60601

   11. Craig Dellimore
       WBBM News Radio 78
       630 N. McClurg Ct.
       Chicago, Illinois 60611

   12. Chief Judge Herman Haase
       12th Judicial Circuit
       14 W. Jefferson St.
       Joliet, Illinois 60434

13. Tim Placher, Attorney
    5 E. Van Buren St.
    Joliet Illinois 60431

14. Lea Drell, Attorney
    54 N. Ottawa
    Joliet, Illinois 60632

15. Tina Brault
    Juvenile States Attorney
    14 W. Jefferson St.
    Joliet, Illinois 60432

16. J. Kevin Davis, Attorney
    168 N. Ottawa St.
    Joliet, Illinois 60432

27.1 Appeal to The Illinois Supreme Court

	)
JAMES ROBINSON	)
	)
Plaintiff,	)
	)
V.	) 94 J 13174
	)
DCFS	)
Defendant.	)

APPEAL TO THE ILLINOIS SUPREME COURT
ON A PETITION TO TERMINATE
THE WARDSHIP OF THE COURT

Now comes the Plaintiff, James Robinson, in his appeal of A Petition to Terminate The Wardship of the Court for Noah Bishton, and states:

1.   Jurisdiction is granted under provisions that allow direct appeal from Circuit Courts where a statute of The United States, or the state has been held invalid.

APPEAL TO VACATE THE ILLEGAL COURT ORDER

2.   That on 7/24/95, Judge Cerri of the 12th Judicial Circuit issued an order (insisted upon by DCFS) attempting to coerce Plaintiff to attend

counseling described as "to better understand the nature of (her) disabilities, and the ramifications of these. The counseling would additionally assist him in helping Noah understand (her) and assist (both) in being supportive of her" in order to get custody of Noah.

3.   First, that Judge Cerri's order (insisted upon by DCFS) of attempted coercion; prima facie, invalidates the State of Illinois Constitution, Section 2, which guarantees to citizens "substantive due process" and "the right to be free from unwarranted government coercion."

4.   Second, that Judge Cerri's order (at DCFS' direction) is, again prima facie, in violation of the federal B. H. Consent Decree, Section II.

A. 3., which states that "acceptance of services from DCFS are a voluntary decision on the part of clients."

5.   Third, that the order itself is discriminatory because it would place an arbitrary, capricious and unwarranted requirement on Plaintiff prohibited by the 14th Amendment; and that is expressly what the so- called counseling entails.

6.   Fourth, the order itself, ignores the conflict of interest inherent here in this instant cause because Plaintiff and Defendant are legal opponents and The Good Honorable Judge performed the action they had requested, and put them in charge over the process even though they are being sued here for violating state, federal and other laws; and it is like putting the wolves who have attacked the lambs to watch over the lambs.

CIRCUIT COURT ORDER AND DCFS
POSITION LACKS MERIT

7.   And, that if counseling intends to increase Plaintiff's psychological knowledge, as stated, it would, if optimum, be redundant, and coercive because Plaintiff completed a book on psychology within the last few months, and will, only increase any knowledge in that field as he sees fit.

8.   That Plaintiff's objections to the unwarranted government coercion by DCFS have been well documented on 12/5/94, 10/18/94, 6/15/95, 6/23/95, 7/3/95, and at other times.

DCFS IS IN SUBSTANTIAL VIOLATION OF FEDERAL LAW

9.   The Defendant DCFS has violated provisions of the USA Constitution, as follows:

10. That Defendant DCFS has released other children to non- African American parents whose knowledge about psychology was considerably less than, or not equal to Plaintiff's.

11. That DCFS's initial coercive efforts after 9/21/94, to force Plaintiff to take parenting classes and an evaluation are additional instances of a). unwarranted government coercion and b). a violation of the B. H. Consent Decree.

12. That DCFS has further misused the psychological evaluation to subvert and undermine plaintiff's rights to custody in a manner similar to illegal literacy tests, or poll taxes and these are like road blocks and obstacles meant to deny Plaintiff citizenship rights.

13. That on 9/21/94, Charlene Necco stated to Plaintiff and Tonya Robinson that it was the policy of DCFS to keep families together, and that "there would be an effort to keep Noah and his brother together" and she has accordingly proceeded in violation of federal laws against age discrimination, and with racially based discrimination.

14. That DCFS has violated due process and equal protection provisions of federal law on 6/23/94, 8/23/94, 9/21/94, and on other occasions.

BABY RICHARD PROVISIONS DEMONSTRATE
AN UNALIENABLE RIGHT

15. That DCFS has violated the "Baby Richard" federal provisions that state that you cannot take custody of a child from a parent unless he is unfit, and you cannot deny custody to a parent who pursues his rights within 30 days after the birth of the child.

16. That a child is a precious gift from God and nature to the parent for custody, guardianship, companionship, and the exchange of love and affection; and the appearance is for the purpose of lessons to be learned, for the child and the parent.

17. That this natural custody and guardianship derives from the fact that the child possesses all the inherited biological memory of the parent from the infinite past, and represents the hope of inheritance into the infinite future.

18. And that in addition to Baby Richard provisions this natural custody cannot be denied, subverted, or compromised except where there are compelling reasons showing that the parent is unfit.

19. That natural custody and guardianship takes precedence over the interposition of the state, especially where the state authorities (DCFS) show intellectual dishonesty, moral depravity, and mental dysfunction.

B. H. CONSENT DECREE VIOLATIONS

20. That DCFS has violated provisions of The federally mandated B. H. Consent Decree as follows:

21. That DCFS failed to make a proper Initial Assessment concerning Noah and his father from the time that Noah was 8 days old, and also violated due process and equal protection.

22. DCFS failed to make a proper Initial Administrative Case Review (ACR) when Noah had been in custody 45 days, violating due process and equal protection.

23. DCFS failed to include Noah's father in the 30 day Case Plan in violation of due process and equal protection.

24. Likewise, DCFS failed to include Noah's father in the Comprehensive Case Plan in violation of due process.

DID THE FATHER EVER HAVE CUSTODY?

25. From the time that Noah was 18 days until he was 81 days old (on June 23, 1994), Noah had unrestricted time with his father, which was and is legal because there is no reason he should have been restricted.

WHEN DCFS TOOK ILLEGAL CUSTODY

26. Then, on 6/23/94, DCFS started restricting the father's access to his own son in violation of "Baby Richard" provisions, and he was not allowed overnight access (visitation).

27. On 9/21/94, Charlene Necco, of DCFS, cut the father's visitation down to 1 hour of supervised visit in violation of Baby Richard provisions, and as an act of Retaliation for the father stating in court what he had been saying from the time Noah was 8 days old- that he wanted full custody of Noah.

28. On about 9/23/94, Charlene Necco coercively arranged for the parenting class and arranged for the psychological testing in violation of due process and The B. H. Consent Decree (II. A. 3.) which states that "acceptance of services from DCFS are a voluntary decision on the part of clients."

29. Charlene Necco has violated The B. H. Consent Decree which requires identifying children who can be returned home (ACR reduction).

30. That DCFS has violated Consent Decree provision I. 14. a., which states that "the components of the Comprehensive Assessment shall all be performed by qualified personnel."

31. That DCFS violated Consent Decree provision I. 15. d., on about 12/5/94 and 6/15/95, in that DCFS did not provide a copy of the case plan two days in advance of the Administrative Case Review, but instead provided them at the actual meeting.

32. On 10/3/94, Charlene Necco said she had 144 cases in possible violation of B. H. Consent Decree case load limits, but this is uncertain because she is a pathological liar.

33. That DCFS has violated the B. H. Consent Decree provision III. 36. a. (4) which requires being sensitive to Noah's "cultural, religious, ethnic, and racial heritage" because Noah is from a healthy, moral, Muslim heritage, and his-placement is not into that kind of environment.

34. That DCFS has-never developed a Reunification Plan for Noah in violation of the B. H. Consent Decree I. 14. b. (2) because he was kept in custody illegally by DCFS since he was about 8 days old.

35. That DCFS conducted a "home study" on Plaintiff in about August, 1994, but it was never fully processed in violation of B. H. I. 14. a., and the study was illegal anyway because their custody of Noah is illegal.

36. That the "objective" listed on CFS 497 for 6/15/95 states "To show interest in children's welfare" and is a display of gross incompetence and negligence from DCFS.

37. That DCFS tried unsuccessfully to coerce Plaintiff into counseling beginning, on 6-15-95 and should have known that their "counseling" coercion was illegal, immoral, and intellectually dishonest because there is and was absolutely no reason for it.

38. That DCFS first tried to blame this "recommendation" for counseling on Dr. Zediker, (beginning on 6/15/95) but their sleazy efforts were detected and the efforts failed.

39. Then, DCFS prevailed on Judge Cerri to order "counseling" to have Noah returned to his father in violation of the B. H. Consent Decree and state law.

40. Then, Charlene Necco sent Plaintiff a highly tyrannical letter dated 7/24/95 (ATTACHED, EXHIBIT A) which says, "As you see, he (Judge Cerri) is (illegally) ordering you to go into counseling as recommended by Dr. Zediker."

131

41. Also, Plaintiff appealed his Service Plan of 6/15/95, (on 6/23/95) which did not show plans to hand over custody of Noah to him.

42. That Matthew E. Franklin, Acting Chief Administrative Law Judge, replied to Plaintiff's Service Appeal - (in a letter dated 8/3/95) stating that Judge Cerri's (illegal) order of 7-24-95 prevented DCFS from directing their office in Joliet from going to Judge Cerri and requesting that the (illegal, immoral) order be vacated; and it is another display of intellectual dishonesty and an inability to choose what is right over what is wrong (moral depravity). See Exhibit B.

43. That DCFS's intellectual dishonesty, obstruction and cover-up is like that of the depraved defective who kills his parents and then asks the court to have mercy on him because he is an orphan; so DCFS is now engaged in tying their own hands, and then saying they cannot do anything because their hands are tied (but they tell lies, (half-truths), they cover-up, and they discriminate to get that effect).

44. That Charlene Necco has demonstrated possible phobic reactions, and the presence of cognitive and affective disorders on 7/3/95, and other inappropriate behavior on 10-03-94, and at other times, in violation of the requirement to have services administered by qualified personnel.

45. That Plaintiff petitioned DCFS on 6/23/94, 9/21/94, 10/14/94, 10/18/94, 12/5/94, 12/30/94, 6/15/95, 7/3/95, and at many other times and (like Thomas Jefferson said), "in every stage of these Oppressions, (I) have petitioned for redress in the most humble terms: (My) repeated petitions have been answered by repeated injury; and a Prince (DCFS) whose character is thus marked by every act which may define a tyrant is UNFIT to be the ruler (guardian) of a free people (children)."

46. And that the chronic deficiencies of DCFS show that DCFS is too much like the Prince of Darkness, full of lies, and wrong doing, despite repeated Consent Decrees.

47. And DCFS is behaving, like Mr. Lincoln would say, "a social, moral, and political evil," just like slavery, because they TRAFFIC IN CHILDREN for their economic livelihood and they exploit and manipulate those innocent children and those chained in poverty and miseducation, and they are COERCIVE tyrants and OPPRESSORS, bartering away children into substitute care for stipends, and pay checks,

and caseloads, like vultures of a sick society; and DCFS must be dismantled as soon as possible.

Wherefore, Plaintiff requests this court enter a judgment against the Defendant for repeated and willful violations of the law, including that relating to custody, age, equal protection, and retaliation. Plaintiff also requests judgment against the Defendant for reasonable attorneys' fees, court costs, and to such other relief as the court deems just.

Respectfully Submitted,
James L. Robinson

28 THE REBIRTH OF THE USA

The USA is very special and unique. It got authorization and validation for its existence through its Declaration of Independence, and then the US Constitution, of 1789 and subsequent amendments. These documents created a covenant containing the USA ideas, ideals, "Mission Statement," and infrastructure. For the USA is a reflection, or image of Ancient Israel. Compare the 42 Prophet-Kings, Philosopher-Priests, from Abraham to Christ, (in the books of Matthew and Luke) with the 42 presidents of the USA. (Note: George W. Bush compares to a post-covenant era president.)

The real world implementation of the covenant falls far short of its ideals! Whatever has a beginning also has an end! So this era is ending, dramatized by the 911 Attacks , and subsequent events and activities. The covenant ended during the presidency of Bill Clinton.

The Rebirth will be implemented based, in part, upon certain principles and precedents, referenced to in the Bible, Qur'an, and Torah. These and other references instruct, inform, and guide our actions. They form the basis for our ideology, motivations, and mission.

The Rebirth of the USA will substantially change the economic, social, political, and military conditions in the USA (and the world) - and the world will experience a Rebirth! We expect the changes to begin in dramatic and significant ways at any time now. But a lot of change will be subtle and gradual.

Here, let me remind you:

I discovered that Thomas Jefferson is the reincarnation of Jacob on 2/23/2002.

I discovered that Prophet Muhammad is the reincarnation of Moses on 5/2/2000.

I discovered information regarding the reincarnation of Thomas Jefferson on 8/4/1999. Youssef Khalim is the reincarnation of Thomas Jefferson.

I had a dream in June, 2008, indicating that Barack Obama is the reincarnation of Abraham Lincoln.

29 SOME SYNCHRONICITY

Chicago was founded by Jean Batiste DuSable after 1764 and before 1776. In 1955, my family moved to Chicago. The 1967 edition of the World Book Encyclopedia lists the area of Chicago as 227 square miles (page 336). Note: Spiritually, "227" is basically the same as "722."

First we lived at 1722 W. Roosevelt Rd. (named for Theodore Roosevelt). The First school I attended was Thomas Jefferson Elementary School, still located at 1522 W. Fillmore Ave., exactly 2 blocks east, and about 1 block north of 1722 W. Roosevelt Rd.

My son, Jimmy Jr., was born on 7/22/68. My father, Samuel, was born 2/22/1909, (similar "spiritual" value, involving the planet Venus). My point: I am associated with Venus (The Morning Star, a "7" or "2"), and the Sun (a "5").

Later, we lived at 1836 S. Harding. (Note:1836 is an important date in the history of the Jefferson and Hemming family.)

Later still, we lived at 5312 W. Adams Street. My brother, James, once also lived in our building. Adams Street is one street south of Monroe Street, and two streets south of Madison Street. My point? Look at the relationship between Jefferson and his two successors. Madison was Jefferson's right-hand man for about 20 years. And Monroe was also a direct political descendant of Jefferson.

Also, Thomas Jefferson and John Adams both died on July 4, 1826, exactly 50 years (the Jubilee Year) from the date of birth of the Declaration of Independence.

Monroe also died on July 4, 1831, Independence Day, symbolically emphasizing the "Declaration" connection.

Lewis and Clark are said to have brought back to Jefferson two bear cubs from their explorations of the lands west of the Mississippi River. I live in the city of the two bears: the Chicago Cubs, and the Chicago Bears.

The street adjacent to my work office location is what? Thomas, of course! Etc. (See similar instances of this in *Healing Begins With The Mind.)*

I believe that Alexander, the Great is one of our guys. It is said that he is mentioned in the Qur'an at 18:83, and is called the Two-Horned One. The Two-horned Sears Tower, John Hancock Center, and some other symbols reinforce this notion. The USA is a renewal of Greece and Rome. We will have to exorcise the residue of the evils of slavery, colonialism, and imperialism from our societies. We were responsible for instituting these diabolical practices sometime in our prior and/or current societies.   135

You see my point:? Individuals exhibit something that I call a soul-print. They operate similar to an atom. They gather around existing conditions, and/or conditions gather around them – that reproduce circumstances, relationships, and experiences during previous lives or existences, similar to the way atoms pick-up, share, or give-up electrons.

30 HOW LOVE WORKS

Note: I'm not sure where the article below came from.

1.   There are, of course, several kinds of love. The kind of love under discussion here is the *love between a man and a woman.*

2.   There are a number of chemicals, or hormones associated with love:

a.   Pheromones: In the animal world, pheromones are individual scent "prints" found in urine or sweat that dictate sexual behavior and attract the opposite sex. They help animals identify each other and choose a mate with an immune system different enough from their own to ensure healthy offspring.

b.   Oxytocin is released when having sex. The hormone has been shown to be "associated with the ability to maintain healthy inter-personal relationships and healthy psychological boundaries with other people." When it is released during orgasm, it begins creating an emotional bond — the more sex, the greater the bond. Oxytocin is also associated with mother/infant bonding, uterine contractions during labor in childbirth and the "let down" reflex necessary for breastfeeding.

c.   Vasopressin is released when having sex. It is an antidiuretic hormone, a chemical that has been associated with the formation of long-term, monogamous relationships.

d.   Endorphins are released when having sex. The body's natural painkillers, they also play a key role in long-term relationships. They produce a general sense of well-being, including feeling soothed, peaceful and secure. They are also released during physical contact, exercise and other activities. Endorphins induce a "drug-like dependency."

e.   Testosterone plays a role in the sex drive.

f.   Estrogen plays a role in the sex drive.

g.   **Dopamine** is thought to be the "pleasure chemical," producing a feeling of bliss. This chemical produces elation, intense energy, sleeplessness, craving, loss of appetite, and focused attention. Dopamine is also associated with states of euphoria, craving and addiction. High levels of dopamine are also associated with norepinephrine, which heightens attention, short-term memory, hyperactivity, sleeplessness and goal- oriented behavior.

h.   **Norepinephrine** is similar to adrenaline and produces the racing heart and excitement. This chemical also produces elation, intense energy, sleeplessness, craving, loss of appetite and focused attention.

i. **Phenylethylamine**, one of the chemicals the body produces naturally when you're in love; is contained in chocolate.
j. **Serotonin**: Researchers found that people in love have **lower levels of serotonin** and also that neural circuits associated with the way we assess others are suppressed. These lower serotonin levels are the same as those found in people with obsessive-compulsive disorders, possibly explaining why those in love "obsess" about their partner.

3.   **There are three distinct types or stages of "love":**

a.   Lust, or erotic passion
b.   Attraction, or romantic passion
c.   Attachment, or commitment

Lust evolved for the purpose of sexual mating, while romantic love evolved because of the need for infant/child bonding. When all three of these happen with the same person, you have a very strong bond. Sometimes, however, the one we lust after isn't the one we're actually in love with. When attraction, or **romantic passion**, comes into play, we often lose our ability to think rationally — at least when it comes to the object of our attraction. The old saying "love is blind" is really accurate in this stage. We are often oblivious to any flaws our partner might have. We idealize them and can't get them off our minds. This overwhelming preoccupation and drive is part of our biology. The attachment, or commitment, stage is love for the duration. You've passed fantasy love and are entering into real love. This stage of love has to be strong enough to withstand many problems and distractions. Studies by University of Minnesota researcher Ellen Berscheid and others have shown that the more we **idealize** the one we love, the stronger the relationship during the attachment stage.

We are attracted to a partner based on appearance, personality (sense of humor, likes and dislikes), and Pheromones.

Love Junkies

There are those who may be addicted to that love "high." They need that amphetamine-like rush of dopamine, norepinephrine and phenylethylamine. Because the body builds up a tolerance to these chemicals, it begins to take more and more to give love junkies that high. They go through relationship after relationship to get their fix.

The feelings of passionate love, lose their strength over time. Studies have shown that passionate love fades quickly and is nearly gone after two or three years. The chemicals responsible for "that lovin' feeling" (adrenaline, dopamine, norepinephrine, phenylethylamine, etc.) dwindle. Suddenly your lover has faults.

If the relationship can advance, then other chemicals kick in. Endorphins, for example, are still providing a sense of well- being and security. Additionally, oxytocin is still released when you're having sex, producing feelings of satisfaction and attachment. Vasopressin also continues to play a role in attachment.

Only three percent of mammals (aside from the human species) form "family" relationships like we do. The **prairie vole** is one such animal.

Note: I'm not sure where the above article came from.

31 PAYBACK CAN BE A BITCH

On Sunday, 1/29/2006,
I was ranting and raving about Illinois criminals:
Former Illinois Governor, Jim Edgar,
Charlene Necco, (of DCFS), and other liars and crooks
In the corrupt Illinois Judicial systems of Will and Cook County.

Then, I realized that baby and child theft
Has been an integral part of this nation
Since its beginning. Charlene Necco and Jim Edgar are just
Routine USA crooks, devils, and baby thieves!

Illinois DCFS is a corrupt, satanic monstrosity. Charlene Necco,
Jim Edgar, and the other criminals involved in child- theft, cover-up,
and obstruction are human-beasts, without a conscience - devils, who
will get what they have earned!

Conversely, Thomas Jefferson was a man of integrity, justice,
And fairness - just as he would be today!
Yet payback came to him!

And TJ was a victim of the caste and unjust system of his day.
But he was also an active participant.
Some African Americans of his day
Must have felt contempt, hatred, and hostility
Toward him for "child theft," and/or trafficking in
Babies, children, Men, and women.

WOW! This realization cooled me off!
Also makes me realize how God is forgiveness,
Mercy, love, justice, caring, and sharing.
We all must look in the mirror first,
Be very humble and forgiving ourselves,
Knowing full well that:

Because of things that we have done in this, or past lives,
And things that nations do now, or have done in the past,
Payback can be a bitch!

32 THE SECOND COMING IS A NUMBER OF THINGS

It is a time when science, technology, and innovation create the conditions for "heaven on earth."

It is a time when those conditions and individuals in opposition to truth, justice, caring, sharing, and openness, and privacy will not exist on earth.

It is the beginning of The Millennium, spoken of in the Bible.

It is the time of The First Resurrection. See Revelation 20.

It is the time of The Judgment, and The Resurrection, spoken of in The Holy Qur'an.

It is a time when integrity and truth will be rigorous not only in business, science, architecture, and technology, but also in religion, social relations, spiritual matters, economics, and social policy. Justice and fairness will be integral components, along with truth and integrity.

The Second Coming is like having brunch at *Old Country Buffet*: You can have all that you can consume, all you need, and you are free to have what you want. But you have to pay an entry fee. And the entry fee is quite reasonable. And everyone will participate in a just and fair manner, creating, building, caring, and sharing. Amen.

33. INDEX

34 ABOUT THE AUTHOR, AND OTHER BOOKS

Youssef Khalim obtained Unity in yoga on about 7/20/80. He says, "We will recombine into one faith, Judaism, Christianity, and Islam." He has been able to "see" and experience some amazing information about USA presidents Jefferson, Lincoln, and Obama; and also Prophets Moses, Muhammad, and Solomon - in visions, lucid dreams, and in meditation. Khalim makes reincarnation (resurrection) central again in our western religions. He resides in the Chicagoland area. And he is the father of Tonya, Runako, and Noah. His books are available at: http://amazon.com, http://sunracommunications.com and http://lulu.com

Youssef Khalim's books include *People Of The Future/Day; You Are Too Beautiful; The Resurrection of Noah; You Look So Good; Healing Begins With The Mind; Jubilee Worldwide; Lara, Forever; Tanisha Love; Galina, All About Love; I Call My Sugar, Candie; Natalia, With Love; Svetlana, Angel Of Love; Lori, My Dream Girl; Love of My Life;* and *The Second Coming.*

www.ingramcontent.com/pod-product-compliance
Lightning Source LLC
Chambersburg PA
CBHW031959080426
42735CB00007B/444